SLAVES AND MASTERS
IN THE ROMAN EMPIRE

Slaves and Masters in the Roman Empire

A Study in Social Control

K. R. Bradley

New York   *Oxford*
OXFORD UNIVERSITY PRESS
1987

Published in 1984 by
Editions Latomus
18, av. Van Cutsem, B. 7500 Tournai, Belgium

Published in 1987 in the United States by
Oxford University Press, Inc.
200 Madison Avenue, New York, New York 10016

Oxford is a registered trademark of Oxford University Press

Library of Congress Cataloging-in-Publication Data

Bradley, K. R.
Slaves and masters in the Roman Empire.
Originally published: Bruxelles : Latomus, revue
d'études latines, 1984.
Bibliography: p.
Includes index.
1. Slavery—Rome.   2. Social control.   3. Rome—
Social conditions.   I. Title.
HT863.B72   1987   306′.363′0937   87-15331
ISBN 0-19-520607-X

2 4 6 8 10 9 7 5 3 1

Printed in the United States of America
on acid-free paper

For
Diane Elizabeth

PREFACE TO THE OXFORD EDITION

I wish to express my gratitude to William P. Sisler of Oxford University Press for making this new printing possible, and to the editors of *Collection Latomus* for agreeing to its appearance. The original manuscript was completed early in 1982. Since that time various items of scholarship germane to its contents have been published, and for the convenience of readers I append a supplementary bibliography.

Winter, 1986   K.R.B.

PREFACE

My object in this essay is to offer some broad explanation of how the Roman system of slavery maintained itself in the imperial age, and to describe thereby some of the adverse conditions under which I believe the majority of slaves in the Roman world to have spent their lives. I have not attempted a full history of slavery at Rome (if such is at present possible), but have been more content to try to examine a few facets of the slave experience. Although the views which result are partial, I hope they may prepare for a more balanced understanding of Roman slavery than is often found elsewhere.

I am happy to acknowledge the help I have received as my work has progressed. Drafts of the book were read and significantly improved by John Drinkwater, Erich Gruen, A. N. Sherwin-White, Gordon Shrimpton and Susan Treggiari. While none of these scholars necessarily agrees with all (or anything) I have tried to say, all have given support and encouragement, and for their generosity of time and interest I am deeply thankful. My debts to other scholars who have earlier dealt with the topics covered will be clear from the citations in notes and bibliography. Preparation of the manuscript has been greatly facilitated through the efforts of A. Nancy Nasser, whose superb typing skills have been an enormously valuable resource to have at one's disposal. And completion of the project has been aided by research awards made to me by the University of Victoria.

Special thanks must be given to Marsh McCall, who not only read my manuscript, but also gave help of a more valuable sort ; for the circumstances under which the book was begun proved far from conducive to its rapid completion, and the fact that there is a book at all (whatever its interest) is very much due to a friend's encouragement to press on in times of adversity. The brunt of the burden of that adversity, however, fell upon my wife, Diane Bradley, and it is she who deserves my greatest thanks. Mere words are inadequate to express my gratitude for her noble and patient willingness to endure and to tolerate it all ; and through the dedication of my book I offer what can never be more than a frail token of all I owe to her. Finally I wish to thank the editors of *Collection Latomus* for publishing my work in their series of monographs.

Spring, 1982   K.R.B.

CONTENTS

ABBREVIATIONS

Authors and works are cited in ways which should be easily understood. The following list comprises abbreviations used for legal, inscriptional and papyrological sources, for journals and works of reference.

AE	*L'Année épigraphique.*
AJAH	*American Journal of Ancient History*
AJP	*American Journal of Philology*
ANRW	*Aufstieg und Niedergang der römischen Welt*, ed. H. Temporini
BGU	*Aegyptische Urkunden aus den Staatlichen Museen zu Berlin, Griechische Urkunden*
CAH	*Cambridge Ancient History*
CE	*Chronique d'Egypte*
CIL	*Corpus Inscriptionum Latinarum*
CJ	*Codex Iustinianus*
Coll.	*Collatio Legum Mosaicarum et Romanarum*
CP	*Classical Philology*
CPL	*Corpus Papyrorum Latinorum*, ed. R. Cavenaile
CQ	*Classical Quarterly*
CSCA	*California Studies in Classical Antiquity*
CTh.	*Codex Theodosianus*
Dig.	*Digesta Iuris Romani*
FIRA	*Fontes Iuris Romani Anteiustiniani*[2], ed. S. Riccobono *et al.*
HSCP	*Harvard Studies in Classical Philology*
ILS	*Inscriptiones Latinae Selectae*, ed. H. Dessau
Instit.	*Institutiones Iustiniani*
JAC	*Jahrbuch für Antike und Christentum*
JEA	*Journal of Egyptian Archaeology*
JRS	*Journal of Roman Studies*
LCL	Loeb Classical Library
MAAR	*Memoirs of the American Academy at Rome*
P. Ant.	*The Antinoopolis Papyri*, ed. C. H. Roberts *et al.*
Pap. Lugd. Bat.	*Papyrologica Lugduno-Batava*
Paul. Sent.	*Pauli Sententiae*
P. Bour.	*Les Papyrus Bouriant*, ed. P. Collart

PBSR	*Papers of the British School at Rome*
PCPhS	*Proceedings of the Cambridge Philological Society*
P. Dura	*The Excavations at Dura-Europos ... Final Report V*, Part 1, *The Parchments and Papyri*, ed. C. Bradford Welles *et al.*
P. Fouad.	*Les Papyrus Fouad I*, ed. A. Bataille *et al.*
P. Grenf.	*New Classical Fragments and Other Greek and Latin Papyri*, ed. B. P. Grenfell, A. S. Hunt
P. Hamb.	*Griechische Papyrusurkunden der Hamburger Staats- und Universitätsbibliothek I*, ed. P. M. Meyer
PIR	*Prosopographia Imperii Romani*
P. Lips.	*Griechische Urkunden der Papyrussammlung zu Leipzig*, ed. L. Mitteis
PLRE	*The Prosopography of the Later Roman Empire I*, ed. A. H. M. Jones *et al.*
P. Meyer	*Griechische Texte aus Äegypten*, ed. P. M. Meyer
P. Mich.	*Papyri in the University of Michigan Collection*, ed. C. C. Edgar *et al.*
P. Oxy.	*The Oxyrhynchus Papyri*, ed. B. P. Grenfell *et al.*
P. Ross.-Georg.	*Papyri russicher und georgischer Sammlungen*, ed. G. Zereteli *et al.*
P. Ryl.	*Catalogue of the Greek Papyri in the John Rylands Museum, Manchester*, ed. A. S. Hunt *et al.*
PSI	*Papiri greci e latini*, ed. G. Vitelli *et al.*
P. Strass.	*Griechische Papyrus der Kaiserlichen Universitäts- und Landesbibliothek zu Strassbourg*, ed. F. Preisigke
P. Tebt.	*The Tebtunis Papyri*, ed. B. P. Grenfell *et al.*
P. Wisconsin	*Papyri at the University of Wisconsin*
P. Vindob. Boswinkel	*Einige Wiener Papyri (Pap. Lug. Bat. II)*, ed. E. Boswinkel
RD	*Revue historique de droit français et étranger*
RE	*Real-Encyclopädie der classischen Altertumswissenschaft*
REL	*Revue des études latines*
RSA	*Rivista storica dell'antichità*
SB	*Sammelbuch griechischer Urkunden aus Äegypten*, ed. F. Preisigke, *et al.*
SO	*Symbolae Osloenses*
SPP	*Studien zur Palaeographie und Papyruskunde*, ed. C. Wessely

StudClass	*Studii Classice*
TAPA	*Transactions of the American Philological Association*
ZPE	*Zeitschrift für Papyrologie und Epigraphik*
ZSS Rom. Abt.	*Zeitschrift des Savigny-Stiftung für Rechtsgeschichte, Romanistische Abteilung*

INTRODUCTION

The purpose of this study is to explore some of the means by which slaves were controlled by their masters in the imperial period of Roman history and to define some of the conditions under which slaves spent their lives as a result. Since the very concept of control is related to the question of the long duration of slavery as an institution in the Roman world, and since Rome can be called a genuine slave society from the third century B.C. (¹), the subject undoubtedly requires examination from a Republican as well as an imperial perspective (²). But concentration on the imperial period alone seems legitimate in view of the fact that Roman slavery, as much else, was affected and altered by the arrival, with Augustus, of imperial peace, so that in what follows the approximate chronological limits of enquiry are marked by the reigns of Augustus and Constantine (³). Even for this timespan, however, some explanation is required for the practical maintenance of slavery over time.

It must be stated at once that the picture of servile life to be drawn is impressionistic and partial : impressionistic because many of the topics discussed could be better understood if the evidence available were capable of quantitative measurement, which is not usually the case ; and partial in the sense that the study will deliberately dwell on the negative side of the slave-master relationship. It is of course very true that at times slaves and masters in Roman society enjoyed a surprising degree of intimacy (⁴), and that simple, constant animosity between slave and slave-owner is too naive a concept to have had universal applicability or meaning. But although the harmonious relations attested between some slaves and their masters should not be lost sight of, they were not in all

---

(1) Cf. Finley (1973), 69 ; Hopkins (1978), 99ff. ; Finley (1980), 86. On slavery at Rome before the third century see particularly Watson (1975), 81ff.

(2) The statement at Plaut. *Curc.* 300, *ita nunc seruitiumst : profecto modus haberi non potest*, contains in my view a fundamental insight.

(3) I stress the word 'approximate' because evidence from beyond these limits will be freely used when considered appropriate.

(4) Treggiari (1975), 48ff. ; Vogt (1975), 103ff.

likelihood characteristic of the Roman slavery system as a whole ([5]). Thus attention will focus on what is conceived to be the essential brutality of the slave experience in the Roman world and especially on the kinds of harsh pressures to which slaves were constantly exposed as a normal part of their everyday lives. There is a danger here that moral judgement on the Roman practice of slavery may seem implied, but such is not consciously intended. Rather the historical reality of Roman slavery must be understood for what it was : to the extent that many of the accomplishments of the upper classes depended upon the leisure time which accompanied the exploitation of a servile labour force, slavery was a fundamental component of Roman society ([6]), and in order to put aristocratic accomplishments into perspective it is vital to understand something of the less elevated, less humane side of Roman social relations, of which the depressed conditions under which most slaves lived provide abundant illustration.

No attempt will be made to give a narrative history of slavery under the Roman Empire. Thus it is necessary by way of introduction to delineate some general features of the Roman slavery system and to make clear some assumptions about it so that they can be kept in mind as the main object is pursued.

Under the Roman Empire slavery did not remain a static institution. Among historians there is general agreement that after the great Republican wars of expansion, first in Italy and then in the Mediterranean world at large, as a result of which huge numbers of war captives were brought to Italy as slaves for use predominantly in agriculture and pastoral farming but also increasingly for domestic service, the imperial period gradually gave way, as wars of conquest declined in frequency, to a system whereby slaves were either bred domestically or else were supplied by dealers (in order to keep up numbers), until both numbers and

---

(5) See in general FINLEY (1980), 93ff. ; TREGGIARI (1979a), 73ff. illustrates the complexity of owners' attitudes towards human property which might occur.

(6) This is not to imply that the Roman world was overwhelmingly dependent on slave labour to the exclusion of other types of compulsory labour, or that other social groups were free from control exercised from above. These are not matters of concern here, however, despite their importance otherwise and will be omitted ; and since the primary emphasis of study falls on slavery as a social institution, detailed economic questions are also omitted. On the profitability of slavery, however, see WHITE (1970), 370 ; FINLEY (1976), 821 ; (1980), 91 ; cf. HOPKINS (1978), 106ff.

the institution itself withered in late antiquity [7]. This dynamic element in the history of slavery is important and the social relations with which this study is concerned were affected by it. But the decline in slave numbers and the withering of the institution should not be exaggerated [8], so that attention here will be devoted to the interaction over time between slaves and masters in what is considered to be a firm, enduring system.

The neat cleavage between masters and slaves, between those who were free and those who were not, should not lead to any belief that slaves in the Roman world ever formed a rigid social class, in the modern sense of that term, with a recognisable consciousness of itself and a concomitant programme for its own amelioration [9]. An enormous variety of functions in enormously different circumstances was performed by slaves, perhaps the most miserable being those of workers in mines and mills to judge from descriptions given by Diodorus Siculus and Apuleius [10]. In particular, slave miners seem to have been consumed as so much human energy with little concern for their needs or wellbeing, and life for these people can have been little more than a grim and meaningless existence. At the other end of the scale, however, were the slaves, both male and female, who belonged to the domestic estates of wealthy Roman magnates. In the luxurious townhouses and country villas of the rich, such people were probably better off materially than many of the free poor, while slaves who belonged to the Roman emperor could enjoy both political influence and relatively high social esteem [11]. For some, that is, slavery may well have had distinct advantages [12]. In between the two extremes, slaves provided labour in a broad range of

---

(7) See Westermann (1955), 60ff. ; 84ff. ; Finley (1979), 137ff. ; Jones (1968), 7ff. ; Brunt (1971), 121ff. ; Milani (1972), 193ff. ; Burford (1972), 49 ; Finley (1973), 84f. ; Maróti (1976) ; Hopkins (1978), 8ff. ; Finley (1980), 67ff. ; 123ff.

(8) Cf. Finley (1980), 123f., citing M. Bloch, *Comment et pourquoi finit l'esclavage antique* in *Annales* 2 (1947), 29ff. at p. 30.

(9) Vogt (1975), 83ff. ; contra, D. Konstan, *Marxism and Roman Slavery* in *Arethusa* 8 (1975), 145ff. at p. 169 n. 77.

(10) Diod. Sic. 5.38.1 ; cf. 3.12-13 ; Apul. *Met.* 9.12.13. On mining conditions see Burford (1972), 73ff., and on mills see L. A. Moritz, *Grain-Mills and Flour in Classical Antiquity*, Oxford, 1958, 67f. ; 97ff.

(11) Treggiari (1969), 106f. ; Weaver (1972), passim.

(12) The importance of the guarantees of food and shelter enjoyed by slaves belonging to large households should not be minimised ; many slaves, by virtue of their location in such households, must have been in relatively favourable economic circumstances. But in general terms such conditions do not appear to have encouraged slaves to remain slaves if an alternative were available, as will become clear later.

contexts, agriculture and pastoral farming, industry and commerce, domestic and private service, medicine and education, even, occasionally, the military ; there can in fact have been few economic areas in which labour and expertise were not provided by slaves at one time or another. But because a miner in Spain can have felt little in common with a herdsman in Italy or with the hairdresser of a grandee in the capital, it is clear enough that distinctions of function led to distinctions of status among slaves (distinctions which were reinforced additionally by intense job-specialisation along the servile scale and by differences of origin), and that in consequence no organisation of group solidarity emerged ([13]).

The circumstances of slave-owners varied almost as much as those of slaves. On one level there was the smallscale owner of a mere handful of slaves, something of the norm in the province of Egypt, though common elsewhere too : Horace for example probably had no more than three domestics at Rome and eight labourers, with a *uilicus*, on his farm outside ([14]). On a far different level, however, there was the Roman aristocrat, a man such as L. Pedanius Secundus, a senator of the mid first century, whose domestic entourage alone comprised a minimum of four hundred slaves, or a woman such as the Christian noblewoman Melania, who is said to have owned, in the early fifth century, the amazing number of twenty-four thousand slaves ([15]). Whatever the plausibility of this latter figure, it is beyond doubt that thousands of slaves, scattered throughout the Empire, were owned by the emperor, who was himself the greatest slave-owner of all ([16]). The incidence of slave-owning similarly varied

(13) For specialisation among slave miners see *FIRA*² III no. 105 ; in the rural context, *Dig.* 33.7.12.5 ; in domestic service, TREGGIARI (1975). Cf. CIC. *Para. Stoic.* 5.36-37 and, in general, FINLEY (1980), 77. For the conditions of public slaves see ROULAND (1977).

(14) HOR. *Sat.* 1.6.116 ; 2.7.118 ; *Epist.* 1.14.1. For Egypt see BIEZUNSKÁ-MAŁOWIST (1977), 93ff. ; cf. J. A. STRAUS, *Le statut fiscal des esclaves dans l'Egypte romaine, CE* 48 (1973), 364ff. BURFORD (1972), 50, believes smallscale ownership the norm.

(15) TAC. *Ann.* 14.43.4 ; *PLRE* s.v. 'Melania 2' for the relevant texts. The wife of Apuleius of Madaura, Pudentilla, also owned at least four hundred slaves, APUL. *Apol.* 93 ; cf. 43-45 ; 17 (on small numbers owned). MART. *Epig.* 12.86 mentions thirty boys and girls in one household. For alleged gigantic holdings ATH. 6.272e ; *HA Firm. Sat. Proc. Bon.* 12.1. Cf. H. FURNEAUX, *The Annals of Tacitus²*, Oxford, 1907 *ad* TAC. *Ann.* 14.43.4. Statistics given by ancient sources are notoriously untrustworthy, but there has to be an eventual limit to suspicion.

(16) Since imperial slaves constituted a particularly distinct status group whose circumstances were often far different from those of other slaves they will not generally be considered in this study. For background, see WEAVER (1972) ; BOULVERT (1970) ; G. BOULVERT, *Domestique et fonctionnaire sous le haut-empire romain*, Paris, 1974. Imperial slaves, however, were no less an exploited group despite their difference in status.

from region to region within the Empire, which, from an economic standpoint, cannot be described as a slave society in its totality [17]. Yet because slavery was entirely absent from no province, even such remote areas as Britain and the northerly provinces along the Danube, and because some evidence is available from those regions where slavery cannot be thought to have constituted the principal means of production, there is no reason to avoid provincial situations completely, or such evidence from them which may be of value for comprehending slave-master relations in the heartland of the Empire where slavery did predominate [18]. Problems of control, that is, were not necessarily dependent upon huge concentrations of slave numbers in all places.

In spite of these variables among both slaves and slave-owners it does not seem perverse to examine relationships between the two main groups. The distinction between slavery and freedom was not meaningless, and no matter how relatively privileged some slaves may have been they nonetheless remained the juridical peers of those less fortunate [19]. Indeed, Cicero gives important expression to the idea that whereas slaves

(17) Although there is general agreement that slavery in the Roman world declined during the imperial age, there are insufficient figures available to allow certain knowledge either of the precise number of slaves in any one place or time or of the proportion of slaves in the overall population in any one place or time. For a recent estimate of the situation in Italy in the late Republic see, with reference to previous calculations, HOPKINS (1978), 101 ; cf. 68 (cf. also FINLEY (1980), 79f.) : two million slaves equalling about 35 % of the full population. It may be valid to insist on a minimum slave percentage in the population at large in order to describe a given society as a slave society (HOPKINS (1978), 99 : 20 %) when economic concerns are paramount. But the view taken here is that wherever slavery existed, no matter what the absolute numbers involved, problems of control might be anticipated.

(18) Cf. R. P. DUNCAN-JONES, *Age-rounding, Illiteracy and Social Differentiation in the Roman Empire* in *Chiron* 7 (1977), 333ff. at p. 347 : 'Some of the practices of Roman Egypt reflect and illuminate for us conditions in parts of the Empire where documentation is much less explicit'. The importance of this statement will become clear in subsequent chapters. For information on slavery in some provincial areas see BODOR (1963) 45ff. ; J. J. WILKES, *Dalmatia*, Cambridge, Mass., 1969, 196ff. ; 235 ; A. DAUBIGNY, F. FAVORY, *L'Esclavage en Narbonnaise et Lyonnaise* in *Actes du Colloque 1972 sur l'esclavage*, Paris, 1974, 315ff. ; A. ALFÖLDY, *Noricum*, Cambridge, Mass., 1974, 127ff. : A. MOCSY, *Pannonia and Upper Moesia*, Cambridge, Mass., 1974, 151 ; 216 ; 241 ; 322 ; P. D. A. GARNSEY, *Rome's African Empire under the Principate* in P. D. A. GARNSEY, C. R. WHITTAKER, edd., *Imperialism in the Ancient World*, Cambridge, 1978, 223ff. at pp. 236ff. ; E. M. WIGHTMAN, *Peasants and Potentates : An Investigation of Social Structure and Land Tenure in Roman Gaul* in *AJAH* 3 (1978), 97ff. ; A. BIRLEY, *The People of Roman Britain*, London, 1979, 145ff. ; BIEZUNSKÁ-MALOWIST (1977).

(19) For the juridical situation see BUCKLAND (1908), 2f. ; that situation was an important expression of class attitude. Contrast, however, HOPKINS (1967), 173.

themselves may have been conscious of their own distinct statuses, from the master's point of view they were all servile regardless [20] : the broad categorization could not be altered and was something more than the merely juridical. Moreover, as a form of property, to be set alongside land and livestock, all slaves were commodities to be used to slave-owners' maximum advantage, adding as well to the latters' social prestige if owned in sufficient quantities. No slave, in other words, was exempt from the forces of social and economic exploitation, a notion which is inextricably bound up with the Roman practice of slavery as a whole. Because of this exploitative element, and because slavery by definition is a means of securing and maintaining an involuntary labour force by a group in society which monopolises political and economic power, it follows of necessity that tensions between slave and free could be expected in the Roman world. Hence a need for control mechanisms is also to be expected if the maintenance over time of slaves in coerced subjection is to be explained.

The historian who wishes to penetrate the lives of slaves in antiquity is confronted by an insuperable obstacle : the absence in extant classical texts of anything that can be called a slave literature, works written by slaves or ex-slaves about their experiences in slavery [21]. He is instead under the great disadvantage of being compelled to draw either on sources which for the most part reflect slave-owners' views and attitudes exclusively, or else on terse and often fragmentary documents whose usefulness is circumscribed by the relatively small amount of information they convey (precious as that information is). Consequently many of the suggestions to be made here are expressed tentatively, as little more than suggestions, not because they are unarguable or implausible but because, given the nature of the evidence on which they depend, they are ultimately incapable of full verification. The evidence itself comes from inscriptional, legal and papyrological sources, all of which contain particular limitations as well as the general constraints just mentioned. The literary evidence, for example, tends to be mainly anecdotal, and allowance has to be made for this as well as for the literary genre

(20) Cic. Para. Stoic. 5.36, atque ut in magna familia seruorum sunt alii lautiores ut sibi uidentur serui sed tamen serui ... On Cicero see MILANI (1972), 204ff. and cf. also FINLEY (1976), 819, 'granted that slavery includes a spectrum of types, it is a fallacy to conclude ... that the institution cannot be examined as such'. Cf. below, p. 35.

(21) But see Appendix F.

supplying it. But with caution in mind it has not seemed inappropriate
even to draw on such an author as Plautus to explain some of the
conventions about slaves perceptible in later literature [22]. The papyri
from Roman Egypt can also be useful, not because what may be learned
from them is necessarily relevant elsewhere, but because what may be
learned is suggestive for other parts of the Roman world for which similar
evidence is less copious [23]. The papyri illustrate well the importance of
using material from diverse geographical areas, in spite of the regional
variations outlined earlier, both because of their suggestive quality, and
because slaves throughout the Roman world were subject to their owners'
control. The sources as a whole, no matter what their weaknesses from
the modern point of view, certainly permit something of the problem of
control to be seen, as too the practical solution to it which slave-owners
used. Likewise, the implications of that solution for servile life can be
sensed at least, and it is with an exposition of those implications that the
following pages are concerned.

The historiography of ancient slavery has been traditionally apologetic
in one way or another and it is not until recent times that the realisation
has begun to set in among scholars that there is something distinctly
unpalatable about slavery in antiquity [24]. Indeed in some quarters
apologetic influences are still at work. Two of the chapters which follow
are concerned with the family lives of slaves and the prospects of
emancipation that slaves had before them. Both take a bleak view of their
subjects, and form a reaction against the line of thinking which can
characterise servile familial life as relatively secure and dignified, and
which can regard the achievement of manumission by slaves as a
relatively easy process [25]. Doubtless at times individual slave-owners
allowed their slaves to live in family units and set their slaves free for
what would now be called humanitarian reasons. But if it is kept in mind
that the Roman slavery system as a whole was by nature oppressive and

(22) On the use of Plautus as historical evidence see below, p. 29 n. 33.

(23) Above, n. 18.

(24) The influences affecting the historiography of ancient slavery are set out at length
in FINLEY (1980), 11-66. For the harsher aspects see recently HOPKINS (1978), 118-123 ;
FINLEY (1980), 93-122.

(25) Susan TREGGIARI, "Contubernales" in "CIL" 6 in Phoenix 35 (1981), 42-69 at p. 61
(and cf. below p. 52 n. 18) ; ALFÖLDY (1972), on which cf. now Peter GARNSEY,
Independent Freedmen and the Economy of Roman Italy Under the Principate in Klio 63
(1981), 359-371 at pp. 361-364.

was maintained for the benefit of the privileged only, the behaviour of such individuals appears exceptional and explains little of the actual conditions governing servile family life or servile emancipation on a day to day basis [26]. Moreover, the belief that slaves comprised a labour force easily managed and compelled to work requires examination [27], and this is done at the outset. Whatever the humanitarian concern for slaves occasionally visible, it must be assumed that slave-owners deliberately manipulated the lives of their slaves to a very substantial degree if the system of slavery itself were to retain its exploitative character across time, which it clearly did.

(26) See FINLEY (1980), 122, quoted below, p. 22 n. 6.
(27) HOPKINS (1978), 108 ; 111, quoted below, p. 25 n. 23.

CHAPTER I

LOYALTY AND OBEDIENCE

The Roman agricultural writer Columella provides in his work, the *Res Rusticae*, important information on the subject of how to manage and to treat slave labourers on the farm (¹). His remarks must be set out in detail because the questions which they raise are fundamental for the purpose of this study.

At first sight an apparent humanitarianism emerges from Columella's recommendations on how the owner of a farm should treat his slaves. He urges careful attention to sick slaves on the part of the *uilica*, and recommends the availability of a large kitchen in the *rustica pars* of the villa which can serve as a resting place for the members of the slave household. The individual cells in which chained slaves are housed should be built so as to admit some sunlight, while the *ergastulum*, although subterranean, should be well lit and as healthy as possible. (With the provision, however, that its windows be beyond hands' reach.) Sturdy clothing for the slaves is advised, and the whole *familia* should be allowed to bathe – at least on holidays, since Columella believed frequent bathing to be physically impairing. For the slave *uilicus* even marital life is catered for (²).

Random details such as these afford something of a glimpse of the everyday living conditions of rural slaves in Italy in the mid first century ; and it would be tempting to associate Columella's rather generous remarks which supply them with what has been perceived to be a broad humanitarian concern for slaves in the early imperial period (³). Indeed,

---

(1) On Columella in general see Brockmeyer (1968), 137ff. ; White (1970), 26ff. ; 332ff. ; Martin (1971), 289ff. ; (1974), 267ff., and on slave terminology in the *RR*, R. Günther, *Kolonen und Sklaven in der Schrift 'de re rustica' Columellas* in R. Stier, H. E. Stier (edd.), *Beiträge zur Alten Geschichte und deren Nachleben* I, Berlin, 1969, 505ff.

(2) *RR*. 1.6.3 ; 1.6.19-20 ; 1.8.5 ; cf. 12.3.7.

(3) For example, Westermann (1955), 109ff. ; Duff (1958), 34f. ; Kajanto (1969), 53ff. ; Milani (1972), 200 ; cf. with greater caution, rightly, Griffin (1976), 268ff. and see below, pp. 126ff. Cizek (1972), 49 states that Columella counselled humane treatment of slaves because free society continued to scorn manual labour. This is only true in part.

the source of Columella's attitude has been found precisely in the Stoic influence allegedly exercised upon him by his contemporary and fellow countryman, the philosopher Seneca ([4]). But there is no more compelling evidence for this view than for the notion that Columella and Seneca were on intimate terms ([5]). The possibility of disinterested humanitarianism should never be discounted as a factor which influenced the kindly treatment of slaves when such is visible ([6]), yet the true basis of Columella's recommendations was one very practical in nature and far from disinterested, as his own words make clear.

According to Columella himself sick slaves were to be given medical attention so that they would become more reliable in response, and sturdy clothing was to be provided by the owner of the farm so that his slaves could work every day, no matter how bad the weather. The *uilicus* was to be allowed a wife so that she could, in part, keep her husband in order, while the hands were to be consulted by the owner because they would thereby become more enthusiastic about their work if they thought their opinions actually carried some weight ([7]). In sum, 'Such justice and consideration on the part of the owner', Columella states, 'contributes greatly to the increase of his estate' ([8]).

It is thus quite clear that Columella's recommendations on the treatment of slaves were designed to promote servile efficiency as the key to economic productivity in a situation where the owner's profit from agricultural production was a dominating principle ([9]). Columella recognised the problem of how to extract work from a labour force which was by nature involuntary, and understood that the solution lay in the provision of incentives towards and rewards for good performance from his slaves. Purely and simply, therefore, apparent generosity was in reality dictated by the economic motive of making the farm profitable, and what becomes visible in Columella's work accordingly is a set of variations on the theme of slave manipulation.

(4) CIZEK (1972), 128.
(5) See Appendix A.
(6) What requires emphasis here is the 'sharp distinction between more or less humane treatment of individual slaves by individual masters and the inhumanity of slavery as an institution'; FINLEY (1980), 122.
(7) *RR*. 1.8.9 ; 1.8.15 ; 12.1.6 ; 11.1.21.
(8) *RR*. 1.8.19, Loeb translation.
(9) Cf. WHITE (1970), 26f.

Columella's attitude was by no means unique. He wrote in fact in a long tradition of proposals and recommendations which stretched back through the works on agriculture of his predecessors Varro and Cato ultimately to the *Oeconomicus* of Xenophon, all of which he knew first hand [10]. Varro, for example, had advised his readers in an important section of his *De Re Rustica* that slave foremen on the farm should be rewarded with a *peculium* and at least a semblance of family life ; consultation of the better hands by the farm owner was also suggested as a means of making the slaves believe their master regarded them well ; and a supply of extra food or clothing was intended to restore servile goodwill (*beneuolentia, uoluntas*) at times when harder work than usual or some form of punishment became necessary [11]. In a much earlier age Cato had similarly stated that the *uilicus* had the responsibility of commending good work in slaves so as to elicit the same from others [12]. It was thus a long-time understanding of farm owners that gentle treatment of their slaves worked to their advantage in a very direct way.

The distinction of Columella, however, lies in the fact that he devotes far more attention to the topic of slave management than his forerunners, and he gives advice suggesting a particular need for the application of common sense to such management. Cato's recommendation that old and sickly slaves should be sold off by the owner makes little sense if, like Plutarch [13], one wonders who would be willing to purchase such property, and it is equally difficult to see the point of putting sick slaves on rations, again as Cato had advised [14]. By comparison Columella's recommendation was more beneficial to master and slave alike. Moreover, Columella admits the prospect of freedom for the slave, the ultimate incentive and reward [15], whereas it is significantly absent elsewhere.

Further, there is an urgency about Columella's material on slave management not immediately obvious in the works of Cato and Varro.

---

(10) *RR.* 1.1.12 ; 11.1.5, etc. Columella makes clear that the catalogue of his predecessors was greater than that now available. For the background see BROCKMEYER (1968), 103 ; 137 ; K. D. WHITE, *Roman Agricultural Writers I : Varro and His Predecessors* in *ANRW* 1.4 (1973), 439ff.

(11) VARRO, *RR.* 1.17.5-7. Cf. MARÓTI (1976), 120.

(12) CATO, *De Ag.* 5.2 ; cf. 5.4 ; 5.6

(13) PLUT. *Cato* 4.5.

(14) CATO, *De Ag.* 2.4 ; 2.7 ; cf. ASTIN (1978), 264f., not fully convincing on the reservations attached to the two passages cited.

(15) *RR.* 1.8.19.

He was aware of the dangers of slave ownership, of slaves' potential for revolt, of the need to rule by fear (*metus*) [16] as well as by kindly treatment, and his suggestions assume something of a prison-camp mentality, for all is seen in terms of security, control and containment as far as the servile labour force is concerned. Almost in a preoccupied manner, he states that the cautious master will himself monitor conditions in the *ergastulum*, will even ask the chained slaves how their overseers are treating them, will allow grievances to be expressed, and he writes that ox-drivers and shepherds are to be quartered close together so that they can observe the extent of each others' diligence [17].

If the need for close supervision of rural slaves is made very clear by Columella, one question which is raised immediately by the *Res Rusticae* is whether, in the imperial period, close supervision of non-rural slaves was also considered important and necessary by slave-owners. There is of course no handbook of regulations for the management of a Roman urban household comparable to the *Res Rusticae*. Yet incidental remarks can be summoned from various authors which do indeed suggest a similar concern with slave management in the domestic sector. According to Tacitus, for instance, one of the reasons which lay behind Augustus' institution of the city prefecture was the need to discipline slaves at Rome itself, while the assassination of the senator L. Pedanius Secundus by a slave in Nero's reign produced the argument that slaves in the city had to be ruled by fear, particularly in view of the foreign element [18]. In both instances domestic slaves were the objects of interest. Domestics owned by the younger Pliny were permitted to make their own wills, and his observation of their provisions resulted, so he says, in a certain community of feeling among them [19]. But such a feeling also eliminated potential for unrest. In most general terms, but terms which must be understood to include domestics again, Seneca argued that harsh treatment produced disaffection among slaves and, in rhetorical fashion, he contrasted a more satisfactory past age with the present, when enlightened, humane treatment had made slaves loyal to their masters

---

(16) *RR*. 1.8.17-18 ; 1.2.1. Cato and Varro did of course recognise that supervision was required ; CATO, *De Ag*. 5.1-5 ; cf. 142 ; VARRO, *RR*. 1.13.1-2. Cf. BROCKMEYER (1968), 112 ; BIEZUNSKÁ-MAŁOWIST (1973b), 370f. ; MARÓTI (1976), 117.

(17) *RR*. 1.8.16 ; 18 ; 1.6.8.

(18) TAC. *Ann*. 6.11.3 ; 14.44.5.

(19) PLIN. *Epp*. 8.16.1-2 ; cf. SHERWIN-WHITE (1966), 467 ; DUNCAN-JONES (1974), 22.

even under torture ([20]). Dio Chrysostom will also have had domestics in mind when he offered the injunction, 'The wise master will give orders to slaves that benefit slaves as well as masters' ([21]), a statement in which the realisation is unmistakable that slaves performed better if consideration of their interests were forthcoming on the owner's part. Even Cato had been able to see the practical value to himself of allowing male and female domestics to consort with each other : intransigence in the household was thereby reduced ([22]).

Owners of both rural and urban slaves were thus aware, it seems, that close supervision of their property was required, both to encourage work and to diminish the possibility of servile disaffection. Slaves could not simply be forced to work by virtue of their subject status ([23]), but instead their social contentment had to be secured as a prelude to work efficiency and general loyalty. Columella, it must be emphasised, was writing for an audience which would presumably identify strongly with his remarks on slave management, which, together with the fact that congruent statements appear in diverse authors less directly concerned with the subject of slavery, makes it incontrovertible that slave management was a wide-spread issue in Roman imperial society as a whole.

As noted already, Columella gives some indication of the means by which social contentment among slaves might be elicited : the provision of decent living conditions, of time off from work, the fostering of family life among slaves, the prospect of emancipation from slavery. Such means acted as incentives and rewards in the lives of slaves, and this fact has always been recognised ([24]). But what is not at all clear is how such acts of

(20) SEN. *Epp.* 47.4 ; on Seneca and slavery see MILANI (1972), 212ff. ; GRIFFIN (1976), 256ff.

(21) DIO CHRYS. *Or.* 14.10 ; on Dio and slavery see CREȚIA (1961) ; BRUNT (1973), 18f.

(22) PLUT. *Cato* 21.2, according to which a fee was levied on the male slaves ; cf. ASTIN (1978), 263 for explication.

(23) Cf. HOPKINS (1978), 108 ; 111 : 'slaves ... could be forced to work long hours throughout the whole year' ; '... high productivity which could be forced out of them (i.e. slaves) on larger farms'. These assertions seem to me to gloss over the difficulties of extracting work from slaves. It may be true, potentially, that 'no other system (i.e. than slavery) offers such undivided loyalty as well as such absolute rights of control and discipline' (FINLEY (1976), 819), but potential could only be realised with effort on the part of slave-owners. Loyalty and high productivity cannot be assumed to be naturally forthcoming from slaves.

(24) A complete list of works in which the point has been made would serve no useful purpose, but note especially the comments made by TREGGIARI (1969), 18f. ; WHITE (1970), 352f. (rather inaccurate) ; MARTIN (1974), 290ff. (distinguishing between material

generosity actually affected the daily lives of slaves, especially on those two fronts which may be presumed to have been most important to slaves themselves, and which are introduced by the agricultural authors, their family lives and their prospects of manumission. What was the precise contribution of these inducements to the maintenance of Roman slavery, what refinements can be established, what recourse was available if and when they did not work successfully ? These questions, while forming the basis of present enquiry, are grounded on the belief that a problem of controlling slaves existed in the Roman world, a problem which is certainly below the surface of the material so far presented, but which requires further description before they can be examined in detail. For to assume a problem of control would be legitimate only if tensions, more or less constant, could be demonstrated between slaves and their masters in Roman society, and while it could with all reason be maintained that expressions of the need for slave management of the kind already mentioned are in themselves evidence of such tensions, there is other important evidence to be brought out.

If attention is turned first to the topic of how slave-owners generally regarded their slaves, a beginning can be made with the depiction in literary sources, which of course represent the views of the slave-owning elite above all, of the slave as a criminous being. Columella again offers abundant material on the theme of the essential criminality of the slave as perceived by the slave-owner, and his overall attitude towards slaves is one of disdainful superiority about which there is nothing unusual. In a lament on the condition of contemporary agriculture he states that farming has been abandoned by the landowning class (with which he naturally identifies himself) to the worst of its slaves, as though to the hangman for punishment. He recognises that the *uilicus* had an important function on the estate as far as management of the *familia* is concerned, but he says that he can be effective only insofar as the servile nature allows. The need to have agricultural slaves kept at work in chains and quartered in an *ergastulum* at night causes him no disquiet. Deprecating statements are extended to urban slaves who, Columella says, cannot provide a suitably qualified *uilicus* for the farm because they are too accustomed to the pleasures and vices of the city, of which a lengthy

and psychological encouragement) ; STE. CROIX (1975), 16 ; ASTIN (1978), 262ff. ; HOPKINS (1978), 126 ; 131. W. DEN BOER, *Private Morality in Greece and Rome : Some Historical Aspects*, Leiden, 1979, 225 is overly simplistic.

catalogue is given. He launches into a tirade against the practice whereby the slave doorkeeper of an urban househould controls access to his master and profits from it. And the highest indignity a slave-owner can suffer, Columella remarks, is to grow so old and lax that his slaves come to despise him [25].

It thus causes no surprise that the *Res Rusticae* also gives ample expression to the owner's view of slaves as an intransigent property. The work contains a liberal sampling of the excesses of which Columella considered slaves capable, or which he had himself observed, as the following itemised list shows :

> They let out oxen for hire, and keep them and other animals poorly fed ; they do not plough the ground carefully, and they charge up the sowing of far more seed than they have actually sown ; what they have committed to the earth they do not so foster that it will make the proper growth ; and when they have brought it to the threshing-floor, every day during the threshing they lessen the amount, either by trickery or by carelessness (*uel fraude uel neglegentia*). For they themselves steal it and do not guard against the thieving of others, and even when it is stored away they do not enter it honestly in their accounts. (*RR*. 1.7.6-7, Loeb translation).

These were some of the servile crimes and misdeeds (*flagitia, maleficia*) which Columella elsewhere reports or assumes. Slaves not under the watchful eye of their owner, being corruptible, were more intent on damage (*rapinae*) than farming. The chained slaves used in viticulture had to be sharp-witted in their work, but all intelligent slaves were classed together as wicked (*improbi*). It was the responsibility of the *uilicus* to get lazy slaves to work, to be aware of their time-wasting and delinquency ; and the *uilica* had to be alert for any shirkers indoors. Columella realised that all slaves could not be tarred with the same brush : in his list of the shortcomings of city slaves it is implicit that all were not considered abject, though nothing more than this appears. He showed personal attention (*comitas*) to those who comported themselves well, took note of the greater loyalty of unchained slaves, and saw that some slaves had to be described as industrious and thrifty. But by and large the representation of servile behaviour found in the *Res Rusticae* is in unequivocally negative moralistic terms : apart from *fraus* and *neglegentia*, the actions of slaves

---

(25) *RR*. 1 *praef*. 3 ; 1.8.10 ; 1.6.3 ; 1.7.1 ; 1.8.1-2 ; 1 *praef*. 9-10 ; 1.8.20.

are characterised by greed, cruelty, avarice and idleness (*rapacitas, saeuitia, auaritia, desidia, pigritia*) ([26]).

It must be stressed that it is servile behaviour of which Columella speaks so much and not servile labour, which on the whole Columella must have believed productive enough ([27]). But be that as it may, some explanation is required of why such a negative presentation predominates in Columella's work, and one solution would be to take simple recourse in the longstanding literary convention of the criminous slave ([28]). This, however, merely raises the question of why such a convention existed at all, and to answer that question the origins of the convention itself must be approached.

Negative servile behaviour is first met in Latin literary sources in the *De Agricultura* of Cato and in the comedies of Plautus his contemporary, though in obviously different ways. Several sections of Cato's treatise, for which there were no Latin models, imply that the agricultural slaves with whom he had had personal experience before the work was composed were difficult to contain and that surveillance was imperative ([29]). Flight, fractiousness, mischief, pilfering and perhaps malingering, all are referred to incidentally as marks of the slave but with the cumulative impact of suggesting a general intractability as the slave's chief characteristic ([30]). In Plautine comedy the *seruus callidus* is by common consensus one of the most successful comic figures of all, appearing ubiquitously in the form of domestic slaves ([31]), yet it is equally agreed that the *seruus callidus* is not a stock character taken over by Plautus from Greek comedy, but an

---

(26) *RR*. 1.1.20 ; 11.1.27 ; 1.9.4 ; 11.1.14, 16, 21, 23 ; 12.3.7 ; 1.8.1-2 ; 1.8.15, 18 ; 1.9.1 ; 11.1.12, 19, 25 ; 1.3.5 ; 1.6.8 ; 1.7.6 ; 1.8.17 ; 7.4.2 ; 9.5.2. Pliny's complaint about tenant farmers (*Epp.* 9.37.2, *rapiunt etiam consumuntque quod natum est, ut qui iam putent se non sibi parcere*) is not really comparable (cf. FINLEY (1980), 126) : debt was the motive for the tenants' actions, which cannot have been true of slave workers.

(27) Cf. BIEZUNSKA-MAŁOWIST (1973b), 367. CIZEK (1972), 49 totally misrepresents *RR*. 1.7 as evidence of servile inefficiency, a text which does not refer to *uilici* ; MARÓTI (1976), 121f.

(28) The corollary of this convention was that of the good or faithful slave, on which see further below, pp. 33ff.

(29) Cf. ASTIN (1978), 265.

(30) CATO, *De Ag.* 2.2 ; 4 ; 5.1 ; 67.2 (cf. 66.1).

(31) On the slave in Plautus see E. FRAENKEL, *Elementini Plautini in Plauto*, Florence, 1960, 223ff. (revised edition of *Plautinisches im Plautus*, Berlin, 1922) ; George E. DUCKWORTH, *The Nature of Roman Comedy*, Princeton, 1952, 249ff. ; 288ff. ; SPRANGER (1961).

innovation and creation of his own ([32]). This fact, taken in conjunction with the prevalence of language associating slaves with deceitfulness, suggests that the behaviour of Plautus' slave characters was based on real historical experience of the sort sketched by Cato and which contemporary audiences could be expected to understand ([33]). In other words, while it is of course unnecessary to believe that the schemes with which Plautus' slaves become involved are realistic in any way, the trickery essential to those schemes makes sense only if it were developed from a popular conception that slaves, in reality, were deceitful and conniving, and such a conception can have only derived from the observed behaviour of slaves in everyday life. The troublesomeness which appears directly in Cato has thus been converted by Plautus into innocent entertainment, but for present purposes that hardly minimises the historical substratum from which the playwright was working.

It is true that there are passages in the *Res Rusticae* which stamp Columella firmly as a moralistic writer, working in a tradition not unlike that of Roman historiography. He complains that women in his own day were so given to luxury and idleness that domestic responsibilities had been forgotten, and he offers a recurring idea in Roman literature at large that rural discipline had been superseded by the attractions of the city ([34]). But whatever Columella's debts to his predecessors in the sphere of agronomy in particular or to conventional literary stereotypes in general, a purely literary approach does not provide a complete explanation of

---

(32) This is not to deny that Plautus may have drawn on Greek models ; cf. SPRANGER (1961), 57, 'So darf man wohl mit gutem Recht in dem griechischen Großstadtsklaven den Prototyp des servus callidus sehen'. But the degree of 'inflation' (Fraenkel) seems unmistakable.

(33) Cf. especially PLAUT. *Asin*. 256-7, *serua erum, caue tu idem faxis alii quod serui solent, / qui ad eri fraudationem callidum ingenium gerunt ; Bacch.* 639-660. The vocabulary of deceitfulness in Plautus includes terms such as *mendacium, seruilis schema, fallaciae, fraudatio, audacia, astutia, dola,* etc. The question of realism in Plautus is of course thorny, but there seems to me to be enough of an unchallengeably realistic element to justify the generalisation of the text. The enslavement of war captives, the manumission of slaves, the availability of the *peculium*, the buying and selling of slaves, child exposure, the existence of professional slave dealers, the practice of hiring out slaves – all of these details (and there are more) in the comedies conform with historical reality and serve to establish a sufficiently realistic basis. (Contrast SPRANGER (1961), 52ff.) Cf. D. C. EARL, *Political Terminology in Plautus* in *Historia* 9 (1960), 235ff. for an aspect of Plautus' topicality, and WATSON (1971), 43ff. for use of Plautus as an historical source.

(34) *RR*. 12 *praef.* 9 ; 1 *praef.* 13ff. ; cf. BROCKMEYER (1968), 139 and on similar expression in Dio Chrysostom cf. BRUNT (1973), 10f. ; JONES (1978), 56.

negative servile behaviour, when the stereotype of the slave can be seen to
have had a basis in historical reality and when there is no reason to
assume significant alteration of that reality by Columella's time. In any
case, the *Res Rusticae* is not in the strictest sense a 'literary' work intended
for the personal improvement of its readership, with an inherent
moralistic foundation imposed by the canons of genre. Rather, it is a
practical manual like that of Cato, designed to give pragmatic instruction
to the landowner. As such it deals on a level of everyday reality that only
the technical handbook can, and thus has no need of any formal literary
devices or preconceived notions dictated by convention. Consequently
when Columella speaks of servile criminous behaviour there is no
alternative but to accept what he says as a literally genuine reflection of
his own experiences in agriculture and farm management : criminous acts
were to be expected from slaves because this was in the order of things.
Moreover, if Columella were to be understood by his readership, it must
be assumed that his remarks reflect a widespread difficulty for slave-
owners of containing servile recalcitrance.

It would be tedious to compile a full catalogue of slave-owners'
statements on this recalcitrance. It is enough to point out, when Columella
or Cato (or Plautus) utter such statements, or when Dio Chrysostom
similarly remarks on the anxieties a slave-owner felt over the possibility
his slaves might steal from him or commit some other act of mischief [35],
that expression is being given to slave-owners' tensions about the stability
of the slavery system upon which they themselves economically
depended. There was simply no guarantee that the system could or would
indefinitely perpetuate itself without effort. Furthermore, although the
actual record of servile insurrection in the imperial age is not (as far as can
be seen) very strong, slave-owners were very much alive to the fact that
slave-owning carried with it the automatic corollary of personal danger to
themselves. The famous Roman proverb that the number of one's enemies
equalled the numbers of one's slaves is an important indication of both the
antagonism with which slaves were regarded en masse by their masters
and of the latters' fears for their own safety, fears which were occasionally
realised with alarming effect [36]. Seneca's report of the senate's fearful
dismissal of a proposal that slaves should be compelled to wear distinctive

---

(35) Dio Chrys. *Or.* 10.12.

(36) Festus, *De uerb. signif.* p. 314 Lindsay ; Sen. *Epp.* 47.5 ; Macrob. *Sat.* 1.11.13 ; cf.
Milani (1972), 204.

clothing again illustrates the corporate apprehension about their security felt by slave-owners [37].

To turn to the demonstration of tensions from the opposite side, that of slaves, it can be stated at once that what was regarded by slave-owners as servile recalcitrance or misbehaviour was not necessarily perceived in the same way by their practitioners. Indeed, since it is obvious that slaves were not usually content to remain slaves when the opportunity of freedom presented itself, it is legitimate to believe that 'negative' actions were in fact forms of servile resistance against or opposition to the social system of which slaves themselves were the victims. What avenues of resistance and opposition were in fact available ?

Perhaps the most obviously cogent demonstration of slaves' unwilling-ness to accept their underprivileged status and conditions comes from their occasional resort to open revolt, though in the imperial age, as already noted, this is a very rare phenomenon [38]. In the approximate period from 140 B.C. to 70 B.C. there were of course three major insurrections of slaves with which Rome had to deal, two taking place in the province of Sicily, the third (most memorable of all due to the leadership of Spartacus) in Italy itself [39]. The relative absence of revolt in the imperial age, however, is in itself no indicator of general servile contentment or passivity : revolt incorporated great risks for slaves, was subject to betrayal, demanded great courage, and depended on expert organisation and leadership, a combination of circumstances which did not often manifest themselves. There is reason to believe, moreover, that the eventual scale of the Republican risings was more fortuitous than preconceived [40]. Nonetheless, the possibility of revolt was always available.

---

(37) SEN. *Clem.* 1.24.1, *Dicta est aliquando a senatu sententia, ut seruos a liberis cultus distingueret ; deinde apparuit, quantum periculum immineret, si serui nostri numerare nos coepissent.* Cf. GRIFFIN (1976), 267ff., and for legal texts showing concern with safety see JONKERS (1934), 243 n. 6.

(38) Outbreaks are attested at TAC. *Ann.* 4.27 ; *Hist.* 3.47 ; *ILS* 961, but may have been more common than the sources suggest ; cf. GRIFFIN (1976), 267 and E. A. THOMPSON, *Peasant Revolts in Late Roman Gaul and Spain* in *Past & Present* no. 2 (1952), 11ff. at p. 12 (slaves included in 'peasant' revolts).

(39) For the Republican slave wars see P. GREEN, *The First Sicilian Slave War* in *Past & Present* no. 20 (1961), 10ff. (and cf. *Past & Present* no. 22 (1962)) ; VOGT (1975), 39ff. ; FINLEY (1979), 137ff.

(40) See Appendix B.

Individual acts of violence by slaves against their owners constitute a second category of opposition. The murder of L. Pedanius Secundus under Nero has already been mentioned, but a similar attack on a certain Larcius Macedo early in the second century can also be noted as an example of the extreme lengths to which some slaves were at times driven [41]. Again, however, violent resistance of this sort included danger for the slaves involved and this must have acted as a deterrent against a high incidence of violent outbursts.

A more prevalent form of resistance, and one commonly attested throughout imperial history, was the tendency of slaves to abscond, and nothing illustrates better the lengths to which owners went to prevent flight than the surviving iron collars worn by slaves, which contained instructions for the return of a captured fugitive [42]. Further, in Roman law special rules were addressed to cases of flight by slaves, and in the early imperial period professional slavecatchers (*fugitiuarii*) came into existence to help contain the problem [43]. In spite of its pervasiveness, however, fugitivism also imposed certain risks upon the slaves who attempted it : separation from family members might be involved, for example, while recapture meant certain punishment.

Finally, the type of dilatoriness and poor work performance of which Columella complained so vigorously can also be interpreted as a form of resistance, in the sense of deliberate sabotage by slaves of their masters' property and economic interests. Naturally it is impossible to measure the incidence of such activity, but the frequency with which servile idleness is referred to must be taken as a firm indication of its prevalence [44].

In spite of uncertainties about their exact frequency, all of the activities mentioned are on record (together with other, probably less common acts such as slave suicide) [45] and they combine to show the expression by

---

(41) PLIN. *Epp*. 3.14 ; cf. 8.14 (Afranius Dexter).

(42) See for example *ILS* 8726-8733, and cf. PLAUT. *Capt*. 357 for a much earlier period. On flight in general cf. BELLEN (1971).

(43) When a slave was sold, Roman law required the seller to guarantee to the purchaser that the slave was not prone to running away ; *Dig*. 21.1.1.1 ; GELL. *NA*. 4.21 ; CIC. *De off*. 3.7.1. Surviving documents show that the requirement was maintained ; *FIRA*² III nos. 87, 88. But the law also contained elaborate regulations concerning actual cases of flight ; *Dig*. 11.4. On *fugitiuarii* see D. DAUBE, *Slave-Catching* in *Juridical Review* 64 (1952), 12ff.

(44) In PLAUTUS, *Pseud*. 139-158 ; *Merc*. 715 ; *Most*. 15-33 ; 789 ; *Stich*. 58-67.

(45) HOR. *Sat*. 2.4.78-79 (stealing) ; DIO CHRYS. *Or*. 10.8-9 (self-neglect) ; on slave resistance cf., briefly, MARTIN (1974), 294f. ; HOPKINS (1978), 121. DAUBE (1972), 53ff. puts

slaves of dissatisfactions with the servile condition. In and of themselves they constitute decisive proof of tensions, and it is not too much to conclude that containment of those activities was a constant preoccupation of the Roman slave-owning classes over time and place and for all manner of slaves.

One of the responses of the slave-owning classes to this situation was to hand down from generation to generation a firm view of the kind of behaviour which they ideally desired (rather than expected) from their slaves, a view summed up in the words *fides* (loyalty) and *obsequium* (obedience) [46]. It is self-evident but nonetheless true that if slaves could be kept acquiescent and compliant the privileged world of the ruling elite stood to gain most, so the emphasis in literary sources on servile loyalty and obedience is not at all surprising and comes to take on a certain conventionality [47]. Nonetheless, some of the relevant material requires exposition because the underlying social attitudes form an essential part of the background against which the practical rewards and incentives have to be seen.

An emphatic demonstration of the association between loyalty, obedience and the slave is found in the works of the great historian Tacitus, for it is the maintenance or denial of loyalty and obedience which governs Tacitus' interest in slaves [48]. At the beginning of the *Histories* he writes :

forward the very interesting idea that slaves demonstrated opposition through 'verbal attack' and sees the fables of Phaedrus as significant examples. For the fable as a form of servile self-defence see PHAEDR. *Fab.* III prol. 33-37, and cf. Appendix F.

(46) Evidence on the topic of the faithful slave is compiled by VOGT (1975), 129ff. The following references to *obsequium* in the text are to be distinguished from the legal use of the term as applied to the relationship between freedman and patron, on which see DUFF (1958), 36ff., TREGGIARI (1969), 68ff. ; cf. also below n. 62, and J. HELLEGOUARC'H, *Le Vocabulaire latin des relations et des partis politiques sous la République*, Paris, 1963, 23ff. ; 217.

(47) VOGT (1975), 129ff. is concerned with illustrating the topos of the faithful slave in literature, with showing that some slaves were indeed faithful, and with showing that Christianity introduced resignation to their status among slaves. This, however, does not seem to go to the more important question of why the topos was a topos, i.e. of why so many authors thought it worthwhile enough to include the motif in their writings. The notion of an aristocratic common view of slaves may be of more help here than that (simply) of literary conventionality, not just for the origin of the topos but for its maintenance as well.

(48) On Tacitus and slavery in general see KAJANTO (1969), rather underestimating the importance of the loyalty theme.

However, the period was not so barren of merit that it failed to teach some good lessons as well. Mothers accompanied their children in flight, wives followed their husbands into exile. There were resolute kinsmen, sons-in-law who showed steadfast fidelity, *and slaves whose loyalty (fides) scorned the rack*. (*Hist.* 1.3 translation, K. Wellesley).

Tacitus was not writing for a servile, but for an elite audience, and it is consequently significant that the elite in society had to be reminded from history of the 'correct' behaviour to be cultivated in their slaves : it was important to speak of traditional social norms in order to preserve them in the present and for the future.

Tacitus deals with slaves as the main object of concern in several sections of the *Annals* and *Histories*. Disturbances are described in Italy in the year 16, disturbances caused by a slave's impersonation of Agrippa Postumus. A rebellion of *pastores* in Apulia in 27 is mentioned, the murder in 61 of L. Pedanius Secundus, the appearance in 69 of a 'false Nero', a man who was either a slave or a Pontic freedman. Finally two uprisings are included, one led by a fugitive slave in Istria in 69, the other also in 69 but in Pontus and led by a slave or freedman of the former king Polemo ([49]).

These events were recorded in the first place because they were judged matters of historical importance by Tacitus. But clues from the language he uses to recount them allow something of the aristocratic attitude towards slaves to emerge clearly. The murder of Pedanius Secundus is called an 'outstanding crime' ; a certain sense of relief is apparent in the account of the miraculous termination of the Apulian revolt, 'as if by heaven's gift' ; the adventure of Agrippa Postumus' impersonator is attributed to the 'brazenness of a slave' ; the episode in Pontus allows Tacitus to comment on the treacherousness of barbarians, similar to that of slaves, and the whole tone of the section on the Istrian episode is hostile to the events outlined ([50]). This uniform disapproval of slaves depends on the fact that all the events mentioned are examples of 'non-virtue' ([51]), and they are such because of their common absence of slave loyalty either to individual masters or else to society at large. Tacitus' adverse bias means that no sympathy is extended by him to the slaves' point of view of the

(49) Tac. *Ann.* 2.29-30 ; 4.27 ; 14.42-45 ; *Hist.* 2.8-9 ; 2.72 ; 3.47-48.
(50) Tac. *Ann.* 14.40.1, *insignia scelera* ; 4.27.1, *uelut munere deum* ; 2.39.1, *mancipii unius audacia* ; *Hist.* 3.48, *fluxa, ut est barbaris, fide* ; cf. 4.23, *fluxa seruitiorum fides*.
(51) Weaver (1972), 10.

events described and little attention is given to consideration of servile motivations.

This is not to deny, however, that Tacitus ever portrays slaves in a favourable light. The slave of L. Piso, governor of Africa in 70, who impersonated his master to save the latter's life, is credited with an 'outstanding lie'. When the maidservants of Nero's wife Octavia were tortured for false evidence against their mistress, Tacitus is explicit that some refused to betray her, and one is even allowed a defiant outcry against the infamous Tigellinus. The corpse of Galba, according to Tacitus, was buried by a slave who can only be regarded as dutiful [52]. Tacitean approval of slaves' behaviour is forthcoming here, implicitly at least, but only because loyalty has been maintained by them, no matter what the personal cost involved. Approval thus depends upon the manifestation of a proper moral attitude laid down by the slave-owning establishment, of which Tacitus himself was of course a representative.

Slavery as an institution posed no problems for Tacitus, moral, intellectual or otherwise. There is a firm commitment visible in his writings to the social status quo : slaves owed their first responsibility to their owners and deserved commendation only if this were apparent. If the obligation were not maintained, slaves became the object of criticism without any concern for the human reasons which led to breaches of the obligation. And since slaves constituted the lowest stratum in society there was a strong tendency to equate low with base ; low in a social sense became low in a moral sense, an illogical step but one which reinforced the prejudice, exemplified by the preponderance of unfavourable over favourable slave references, and which permitted no differentiation among slaves [53].

There was in Tacitus' thinking something of a composite, perhaps even stereotyped slave personality, in which certain features − recklessness, cowardice, criminality − are shown as common to all slaves. There is little reason to doubt in all of this that Tacitus departed from views that were typical of his peer group [54], upper class Romans whose wealth and

---

(52) TAC. *Hist.* 4.50, *egregio mendacio* ; *Ann.* 14.60 ; *Hist.* 1.49.

(53) Cf. above, p. 18.

(54) See TAC. *Ann.* 1.17.1 ; 2.12.4 ; 2.39.2 ; 6.10.3 ; 12.4.1 ; 13.46.4 ; 14.40.1 ; 15.45.5 ; *Hist.* 1.46 ; 1.48 ; 2.59 ; 2.92 ; 3.32 ; 5.9. Cf. TREGGIARI (1969), 265ff. for descriptions of freedmen as slaves by Cicero for perjorative reasons. Among historians other than Tacitus, Appian may be noted especially for his interest in servile loyalty and disloyalty. The fourth book of his *Civil War* is replete with late Republican examples of

position in society made them impervious to the circumstances of those less privileged. The book, for example, of Valerius Maximus on memorable deeds and sayings contains a section entitled 'On the Loyalty of Slaves' [55]. In it the author provides a catalogue of examples taken from late Republican history in which slaves demonstrated loyalty to their masters at moments of crisis and at cost to themselves. Possibly the most poignant is the tale of a slave belonging to a certain Antius Restio, who, although previously brutalised (he had been shackled and branded), nevertheless saved his proscribed owner from assassination by building a funeral pyre and burning on it the corpse of an old man he claimed to be his master. To Valerius Maximus, this was an instance not just of *fides*, but of goodwill (*beneuolentia*) and dutifulness (*pietas*) too [56]. A repository of such anecdotes about slaves must have been generally available to writers, because Seneca used the same kind of examples as Valerius to prove his point that a slave could confer a benefit (*beneficium*) on his master [57]. In a totally different context, however, the biographer Suetonius records that the future emperor Caligula, while at Capri with Tiberius, showed so much *obsequium* that he could be described as the ideal slave [58]. In his comparison of Trajan's reign with that of Domitian, the younger Pliny argued that social and moral normality had returned to Rome once the emperor was no longer using slaves as informants against their masters : *obsequium* had been restored to slaves, 'who are to respect, obey and preserve their masters' [59]. According to two passages in the *Historia Augusta*, Marcus Aurelius armed gladiators whom he called the *obsequentes*, and Aurelian discouraged by imperial letter servile obedience among the soldiery [60]. Even under the changing conditions of the late imperial age loyalty and obedience still remained the desired servile ideal

---

both, and Appian's attitude is clear enough : having described Cinna's massacre of slaves who had earlier plundered and murdered, he comments, 'Thus did the slaves receive fit punishment for their repeated treachery to their masters' (*BC* 1.74, Loeb translation). Note also, much later, Amm. Marc. 18.3.2ff. ; 19.9.4ff.

(55) Val. Max. 6.8, *de fide seruorum*.

(56) Val. Max. 6.8.7. Valerius' contemporary, Velleius Paterculus, referring again in a lugubrious passage to events of the late 40's B.C., similarly thought it noteworthy that some servile loyalty had been preserved towards proscribed masters (2.67.2, *fidem ... aliquam*).

(57) Sen. *Ben.* 3.18-27.

(58) Suet. *Cal.* 10.2.

(59) Plin. *Pan.* 42.2.

(60) *HA Marc.* 21.7 ; *Aurel.* 7.8.

to judge from Macrobius, who, in the first book of the Saturnalia, introduced through his character Praetextatus a further string of anecdotes illustrating slave virtues, some of them familiar from previous authors [61]. It is significant that despite their conventionality such stories could still circulate at the turn of the fifth century with their collective emphasis on loyalty and obedience.

The historicity of the stories about slave loyalty and disloyalty which have been referred to is unimportant here. What is striking and worth emphasis is the consistent attitude over time and among diverse authors towards what was thought to be desirable and commendable behaviour in slaves, because that attitude stood for the maintenance of the established social order and against any resistance to it from the servile element. Naturally this attitude catered to the interests of the aristocracy which perpetuated it, and this is one reason why it receives so much attention in literature. Moreover, loyalty and obedience of slave to master was only one form in Roman society, where categories of social status and role were heavily demarcated by patriarchal and aristocratic tradition, of the manner in which obligations were imposed on various social groups. The kinds of family loyalties considered desirable in free society, for instance, are illustrated in the quotation above from Tacitus, while the loyalty of freedman to patron and of wife to husband are analogous [62]. Servile loyalty and obedience, therefore, belonged to a wider nexus of social obligations imposed downwards from the upper levels of society, obligations which of course by the beginning of the period were established concretely. It is the 'correctness' of this behaviour, however, which is the main point.

What effects did the perpetuation of what might be called this aristocratic ideology of loyalty and obedience have ? In many ways servile acquiescence seems to have followed as a matter of course from the mere process of inculcation. The historical cases of maintained loyalty reported

(61) MACROB. Sat. 1.11.16-46.
(62) See DUFF (1958), 36ff. ; TREGGIARI (1969), 68ff. ; BOULVERT (1970), 101 (though Dig. 37.15.9 is inapposite) ; WILLIAMS (1958), 16ff. ; JONES (1978), 24 (on the submissiveness expected by aristocrats from their social inferiors). For the notion of total subservience implicit in obsequium see SUET. Aug. 21.1 (the obedience of defeated enemies) and TERT. Spect. 1 (obsequium as the Christian's obedience to God) ; and on the related term oboedientia see CIC. Para. Stoic. 5.35, oboedientia fracti animi et abiecti et arbitrio suo carentis (defining seruitus) ; cf. 5.41. See also ILS 8034, 8401, 8430, 8430a, 8473.

by Tacitus, for instance, show that obedience was displayed without question by some slaves at some times. More significantly, inscriptional dedications made by owners to deceased slaves who were described as 'most faithful', and dedications to owners set up by their slaves provide a firmer indication of servile compliance over long periods of time, compliance which is underscored by the virtual ordinariness of these commemorative texts [63]. Furthermore, the 'normality' of the slave's deferential attitude towards his master in society at large is well illustrated from Christian, that is non-aristocratic, literary sources. Since Christianity in its earliest stages was a religion which appealed to and spread among the lower orders of society, it is not surprising to find injunctions to slaves from the teachers of the new doctrine [64]. The stress contained in these injunctions on servile obedience is remarkable for a religion which taught the spiritual equality of all mankind, and what this reflects is an unqualified acceptance of the existing social structure in which they found themselves by early Christians [65]. The brotherhood of man inherent in the teachings of Christianity anticipated equality not in the present world but in the world to come, and for slaves the important point was to be able to withstand one's condition and to fulfill its obligations in expectation of a better life ahead. Thus the emphasis beneath the reiterated instruction, 'Servants, obey your masters', was on preserving and reaffirming current social norms, which for slaves was a state of passivity and compliance to the will of the slave-owner. Early Christian literature, it can thus be said, seems to show how ingrained and pervasive this state had become as a result of the steady downward imposition of aristocratic values.

As already intimated, the association of the slave with loyalty and obedience has a long literary history, its first expression appearing again in the Plautine corpus [66]. The *seruus callidus* of Plautus' comedies is

(63) For example, *ILS* 7370, 7371, 7376, 7378, 8421. Vogt (1975), 131, states that 'Educated Roman society was sufficiently open-minded in the second century B.C. to recognize that such devoted servants and assistants possessed that part of the moral personality embraced in the concept of *fides*'. Rather, the aristocratic desirability of *fides* had been created by that date.

(64) *Tit.* 2.9-10 ; I *Cor.* 7.20-24 ; *Coloss.* 3.22-4.1 ; *Ephes.* 6.5-9 ; I *Tim.* 6.1-2 ; I *Pet.* 2.18-20 ; *Did.* 4.11 ; *Barn.* 19.7.

(65) Cf. *Matt.* 10.24-25 ; *Luke* 6.40 ; *John* 13.16 ; 15.20 ; Jonkers (1934), 247ff. ; Ste. Croix (1975). For the revolutionary potential of Christian teaching, J. Morris, *Early Christian Orthodoxy* in *Past & Present* no. 3 (1953), 1ff. at p. 5.

(66) For the type, Spranger (1961), 16. For the language of obedience, note Plaut. *Bacch.* 993 ; *Capt.* 195-200 ; 349 ; 363 ; 428 ; 438 ; 716 ; *Cas.* 449 ; *Epid.* 348 ; *Merc.* 156 ; *Most.* 785 etc.

often a *seruus fidus*, Tyndarus in the *Captiui* perhaps representing the noblest example of the type. It would of course hardly have been appropriate for Plautus to create slave characters for the stage openly inimical to their masters' interests, but servile devotion to their owners must be taken as a reflection of what free society hoped for in reality and sometimes achieved. Yet there is a sequence of soliloquies spoken by slave characters in the plays which are disquisitions, from the servile point of view it must be emphasised, on the meaning of loyalty and obedience, and which are very revealing [67]. Faithfulness and diligence are shown to be not automatic, selfless responses from slaves to their condition, but rather means of avoiding physical punishment or gaining some reward from their owners. In other words, Plautus provides a hint of the disparity between owners' and slaves' interpretations of *fides* and *obsequium*. It is obvious that by Plautus' day Roman slave-owners had created the ideal of loyal behaviour from their slaves, but it would be surprising if slaves themselves had accepted this, and the subservience which accompanied it, as an ideal of their own choosing and without question [68]. The expression in aristocratic literature of a desirable form of servile conduct was after all the expression only of an ideal wish for social stability between slave and free, and it is clear from what has already been said that the ideal did not always coincide with reality. No society in which one section of the population is held in subjection by another can expect social relations to be constantly stable, and that is implicit, for Roman society, in the opening statement of Valerius Maximus' work previously referred to : 'It remains for me to relate the loyalty of slaves to masters, *which is all the more deserving of praise because least expected*' [69].

Incentives and rewards thus functioned as mechanisms for the attainment of the ideal on a practical level. Social stability, as expressed in the moral terms *fides, obsequium, beneuolentia, pietas,* or through the absence of servile *flagitia* and *maleficia,* could be secured by directly catering to and accommodating the human interests of slaves. In other words, the use of incentives and rewards by slave-owners points to a process of social control at work in the Roman Empire, a process which

---

(67) PLAUT. *Amph.* 959ff. ; *Aul.* 587ff. ; *Rud.* 918ff. ; *Pseud.* 1103ff. ; *Most.* 859ff. ; *Men.* 966ff. The significance of the motives expressed in these passages is highly distorted by VOGT (1975), 131.

(68) Note PLAUT. *Asin.* 380, flight as an *officium* of the slave, and cf. above n. 63.

(69) VAL. MAX. 6.8 *praef., Restat ut seruorum etiam erga dominos quo minus expectatam hoc laudabiliorem fidem referamus.*

operated to preserve existing social differentials and which was dictated by the elite, whose object was to create servile loyalty and obedience so that its privileged existence was not threatened from below ; and expression of the object, as has been seen, continued throughout the imperial age. In order to illustrate the meaning of these statements in more detail, one specific type of generosity can be examined, the practice of masters periodically granting holidays to their slaves.

Holidays for slaves are attested from at least the time of Cato until the late imperial period ([70]). The annual number of these occasions was never excessive, but it seems nevertheless to have been fairly well-defined and protected. As a general rule slaves were barred from the ceremonial aspects of religious festivals – the origin of all holidays – because they were thought to be a defiling or polluting influence ([71]). Yet the Roman calendar prescribed nonetheless a specific number of annual holidays from which slaves were not excluded on religious grounds. Thus a holiday was included in the Matronalia of March 1 ; slaves took part in the festival of Fors Fortuna on June 24 ; August 13 was a holiday for slaves alone, not the free population ; and slaves also participated in the two major celebrations at the turn of the year, the Saturnalia (December 17-23) and the Compitalia (January 3-5) ([72]). Moreover in a papyrus apprenticeship contract from Roman Egypt for a female slave about to learn the trade of weaving, a provision is included for eighteen days annual holiday on account of festivals ([73]). A number of other such contracts is known with similar provisions but in which the apprentice is freeborn not servile ([74]). The highest total of holidays allowed in these

(70) What follows is adapted from K. R. Bradley, *Holidays for Slaves* in *SO* 54 (1979), 111ff. ; cf. also Astin (1978), 265.

(71) Plut. *QR* 16 (with Rose *ad loc.* ; cf. *Camillus* 5.2) ; Suet. *Claud.* 22 ; Zos. *Hist. Nou.* 2.5.1 ; cf. Plut. *Aristides* 21.2 ; Ath. 6.262b ; R. M. Ogilvie, *The Romans and Their Gods in the Age of Augustus*, New York, 1969, 91f.

(72) Matronalia : Macrob. *Sat.* 1.12.7 ; Lydus, *De Mens.* 3.22 ; Fors Fortuna : Cic. *De Fin.* 5.70 ; Ovid, *Fasti* 6.771ff. ; August 13 : Plut. *QR* 100 ; Festus, *De Verb. Signif.* p. 460 Lindsay ; Saturnalia : Sen. *Ep.* 47.14 ; Ath. 14.639b ; Iust. 43.1.4 ; Dio Cass. 60.19.3 ; Luc. *Sat. passim* ; Compitalia : Dion. Hal. 4.14.3-4. Cf. in general J. Marquardt, *Römische Staatsverwaltung* III, Leipzig, 1878, 197ff. ; 548f. ; 554f. ; 562ff. ; J. G. Frazer, *The Golden Bough*[3] Part *VI, The Scapegoat* (reprint) London, 1966, 306ff. ; K. Latte, *Römische Religionsgeschichte*, Munich, 1960, 254 ; G. Dumézil, *Archaic Roman Religion*, Chicago, 1970, II 618.

(73) *P. Oxy.* 1647.

(74) *P. Oxy.* 725 (twenty days) ; 2586 (eleven days) ; *P. Fouad* 37 (thirty-six days) ; cf. also *P. Oxy.* 2971 ; and *P. Wisconsin* 5, where a female slave hired out as a weaver is given

documents is thirty-six, but one is close to the arrangement for the slave apprentice and one is lower. If the arrangement for the female slave was common it might be that a greater number of holidays was given to a more valuable or potentially more accomplished slave ; that is, distinctions may have been drawn depending on the status of the slave, for from Varro it seems that the *uilicus* might be more favoured than ordinary hands ([75]), although this cannot be certain.

It is equally difficult to say whether slaves enjoyed holidays other than those already mentioned for which clear testimony exists. For Rome itself the possibilities are governed by the number of religious festivals and of games (*ludi*) held during the year, on which some statistics are available. Through the late Republic and early Empire the number of days marked *feriae* gradually increased until Marcus Aurelius imposed a limit of one hundred and thirty-five, while by the mid fourth century the number of days on which *ludi* were given had similarly increased from seventy-seven in the time of Augustus to one hundred and seventy-seven ([76]). Some of these of course overlapped. Now although legal and other official business could not be conducted on days marked *feriae* most of the free population, especially at the lower levels of society, probably went about its business much as usual ([77]). Even in the case of the free poor a distinction has to be drawn between *feriae* which called for little more than religious observance by priests, and festivals which constituted major periods of holiday. For slaves accordingly it should be true in general that they were required to fulfill their functions on these as on other days. Apart from the matter of their religious exclusion it seems doubtful that they can have shared entirely whatever free time was available at holiday periods, for in the case of the games the full working day was not lost for those who did attend, an obvious limit was set on the number who could attend at any one time, and tickets cannot have been easily accessible to slaves ([78]). If they happened to attend with their owners, this could have meant only a limited form of respite at most.

---

at least eight days holiday a year. Cf. Herbert C. YOUTIE, *The Heidelberg Festival Papyrus : A Reinterpretation* in P. R. COLEMAN-NORTON ed., *Studies in Roman Economic and Social History in Honor of Allan Chester Johnson*, Princeton, 1951, 178ff.

(75) See above, p. 23.

(76) BALSDON (1969), 245ff.

(77) BALSDON (1969), 244 ; cf. BRAUN (1959), 57 ; 68ff. ; 81ff.

(78) BALSDON (1969), 248 ; 268.

For rural slaves it is implied by both Cato and Columella in random passages that local holidays were kept. Columella indeed speaks of a period of forty-five days when no ploughing was possible because of bad weather and holidays as well as a period of thirty days given over to rest once the sowing season was over ([79]). Cato gives a list of jobs which could be done by slaves on local and private holidays, and Columella follows suit, in even fuller detail, with a whole catalogue of chores which, if adhered to, could have produced no more than partial relief from work ([80]). There is no way of telling how representative of other slave-owners' attitudes Cato and Columella were, whether for urban or rural slaves, and in reality much must have depended on the personal inclinations of individual masters. But the demands of labour, especially in agriculture, did not disappear at holiday times and the indications are that slaves enjoyed only a small number of specifically designated days' relief from work.

Two considerations must be made at this point to put into higher relief the unusual character of slave holidays. First, the servile population of Rome and Italy was far greater in late Republican and early imperial times than in the early historical period when the holidays first came into existence ([81]). This being so, it seems rather curious at first sight that a depressed element in Roman society should have been periodically permitted irregular freedom of movement and action when the potential for various unsavoury acts that existed among slaves might be realised. Of special note in this connection is the emphasis found in the sources on the licence (*licentia*) of slaves at the Saturnalia ([82]). Secondly, and in contrast, the holidays continued over time to provide opportunities for the demonstration towards slaves of generosity on the part of slave-owners, apart from whatever free time from work was allowed. At the Matronalia mistresses gave their slaves special meals as part of the holiday, and the same was done by masters at the Saturnalia ([83]). At both Compitalia and Saturnalia even Cato had prescribed an increase of rations for field hands ([84]). Again at the Saturnalia normal restraints were removed from

(79) Cato, *De Ag.* 132.1 ; 140 ; Col. *RR.* 1.8.5 ; 11.1.19 ; 2.12.9 (cf. 11.2.95-6 ; 98).
(80) Cato, *De Ag.* 2.4 ; 140 ; Col. *RR.* 2.21.
(81) See Brunt (1971), 121ff.
(82) Cf. Dio Cass. 27.93 ; Macrob. *Sat.* 1.7.26 ; Plut. *Sulla* 18.5 ; Luc. *Sat. passim.*
(83) Sen. *Ep.* 47.14 ; Solin. 1.35 ; Ath. 14.639b ; Iust. 43.1.4 ; Luc. *Sat. passim.* ; Macrob. *Sat.* 1.7.37 ; 12.7 ; 24.22-3.
(84) Cato, *De Ag.* 57.

slaves to the extent that they might gamble and address their masters more frankly than usual ; and at the Compitalia signs of servitude were removed from slaves [85].

If attention is now turned to accounting for the continued maintenance of these holidays it must be stated first that since all Roman holidays were in origin days of religious observance, religious traditionalism must form part of any explanation. The habits of centuries could not be simply set aside. But it is questionable to what extent by the imperial period the original reasons for all religious ceremonies were remembered or considered valid. It was of course long remembered in Roman lore that the Saturnalia recalled an age of gold during the reign of Saturn when a natural abundance of material needs made slavery an unnecessary institution ; all men were then free and equal [86]. Less assurance, however, is visible in the sources which speak of the origin of the holiday for slaves alone on August 13. This was thought by Festus to mark the foundation of the temple to Diana on the Aventine by Servius Tullius, who had been born a slave, whereas Plutarch believed that the same day commemorated Tullius' birthday [87]. More strikingly, Plutarch was at a complete loss to explain the peculiar hairwashing ritual of women on August 13 : 'Why is it that ... the women are in the habit of washing and cleansing their hair on that day in particular ? ... Did the headwashing start from the slave-women in consequence of their holiday and spread to free women ?' [88] No positive answer can be given. Again, while the ability of slaves to take part in the ceremonies of the Compitalia and of Fors Fortuna was also attributed to Servius Tullius, this does not explain the statement of Dionysius of Halicarnassus that in his day, the Augustan age, all traces of their condition were removed from slaves at the Compitalia [89].

It seems, therefore, that the religious-mythological origins of slave holidays gradually became obscured but, as has been seen, the holidays

---

(85) HOR. *Sat.* 2.7 ; MART. *Epig.* 4.14.7ff. ; 5.30.7f. ; EPICT. *Diss.* 1.25.8 ; DIO CASS. 60.19.3 ; LUC. *Sat. passim.* ; DION. HAL. 4.14.4.

(86) LUC. *Sat.* 7 ; IUST. 43.1.3 ; MACROB. *Sat.* 1.7.26 ; cf. BRAUN (1959), 58ff. ; 76ff. Braun argued that the various taboos associated with all holidays preserved a collective memory of a golden age ; but he gave no evidence of traditional connections between specific holidays and a golden age, except for the Saturnalia.

(87) FESTUS, *De Verb. Signif.* p. 460 Lindsay ; PLUT. *QR* 100.

(88) PLUT. *QR* 100 translated by H. J. ROSE, *The Roman Questions of Plutarch*, Oxford, 1924.

(89) OVID, *Fasti* 6.771ff. ; DION HAL. 4.14.3-4.

themselves were not dispensed with. It is preferable in consequence to set these occasions in the context of master-slave relations outlined above and to regard them as a vehicle of social control, a view for which there is important corroborative literary evidence in Solinus and Macrobius, authors who have explicit statements on the connection between slave holidays and social stability. They remark that slaves were given banquets (*cenae*) on March 1 and at the Saturnalia by their owners in order to foster *obsequium* for the immediate future or as compensation for work completed in the recent past : 'so that at the beginning of the year they might incite their slaves to steadfast obedience through reward' or 'as it were pay off the account for work completed' [90]. Even though these writers were aware of the antiquity of the custom of providing meals for slaves, no religious association or explanation occurs in the passages referred to. Instead what is discernible is a motivation on the part of owners to keep their slaves under control through the use of sparing rewards or incentives. Dionysius of Halicarnassus has a further relevant observation : commenting on the Compitalia he writes that signs of slavery were removed then 'in order that the slaves, being softened by this instance of humanity, which has something great and solemn about it, may make themselves more agreeable to their masters and be less sensible of the severity of their condition' [91]. What emerges, therefore, is a desire by slave-owners to appease slaves, to make the servile condition more tolerable by providing temporary but periodic respites from it.

In summary, then, it has been maintained in this chapter that the institution of slavery presented a conflict between the unwillingness of slaves to accept passively their position of social inferiority in the Roman world and the desire of slave-owners to maintain the institution for their own continuing benefit. Servile opposition to the Roman social system was demonstrated by means of flight, deliberate inefficiency at work and, occasionally, violent revolt, activities which ran counter to the ideal of servile loyalty and obedience which owners handed down from

(90) Solin. 1.35 ... *ut honore promptius obsequium prouocarent ... quasi gratiam repensarent perfecti laboris* ; Macrob. *Sat.* 1.12.7 ... *ut ... ad promptum obsequium honore seruos inuitarent ... quasi gratiam perfecti operis exsoluerent* ; the language suggests either the use of the former by the latter or else the use by both of a common source. These texts seem decisive in establishing a connection between holidays and management ; contrast Milani (1972), 199, however, who sees holidays as a sign of the flexibility of the barrier between slavery and freedom, perhaps too simplistically.

(91) Dion. Hal. 4.14.4 (Loeb translation). Cf. Cic. *De Leg.* 2.19 ; 29.

generation to generation. In order to resolve the conflict, to negate the potential for servile resistance and to achieve the ideal of compliance – in other words, to secure social stability – slave-owners granted various incentives and rewards which catered to their slaves' interests, and, to an extent, diminished the severity of slavery. These included holidays, whose function as a device for reducing tensions between slave and free can be satisfactorily perceived.

In the following chapters detailed examination will be made of how two of the incentives and rewards mentioned by Roman authors, family life and manumission, actually functioned in the everyday lives of slaves. It will then be shown how masters reinforced this system of relatively generous treatment with a constant counterpoint of violence in order to secure their ends. Together the generosities and climate of fear which can be seen to surround servile life help to explain the survival over time of the Roman slavery system.

CHAPTER II

THE SLAVE FAMILY

In the Roman imperial age, as in other periods of classical history, the family constituted the basic social unit among the free [1]. To the elite the traditions of the family and the importance attached to preserving and continuing them were sometimes so strong that it was considered more satisfactory that they be assumed by adopted descendants, if there were no alternative, than that they die out altogether [2]. Given this predominant norm, it could be assumed that slaves would wish to establish and live in their own family units if conditions were to allow, even though marriage between slaves, and hence the existence of a slave family, was technically a legal impossibility [3]. But three types of evidence prove the assumption correct, that from literary sources, that from legal sources, and that from sepulchral inscriptions, the last being especially important since it comes directly from slaves themselves.

Servile familial arrangements are incidentally alluded to in all kinds of literature from the imperial period. Martial, for example, expresses the hope of a lasting union between two slaves about to marry, and Juvenal refers to one of his own domestics as the son of slave parents on his farm at Tibur ; Tertullian assumes the normality of slave marriages in his rhetorical statement that discipline among slaves is better if they marry within the same household, and Ammianus Marcellinus tells of a slave who informed against his master after his wife (*coniunx*) had been flogged [4]. From Christian literature a parable in Matthew's Gospel is worth special note. According to the story a slave unable to repay a debt to his master on request was eventually forgiven, but proved far less lenient in his own treatment of a fellow slave who in turn owed him

---

(1) Weaver (1972), 95. For an indirect affirmation of the value of marriage and family life, see Dio Chrys. *Or.* 7.133 ; 135, on prostitution.

(2) Cf. Veyne (1961), 221.

(3) Buckland (1908), 76.

(4) Mart. *Epig.* 4.13 ; Iuv. 11.146ff. ; Tert. *Ad ux.* 2.8.1 ; Amm. Marc. 28.1.49.

money. Once the master discovered this, he punished the slave. Obviously the story is fictional, but if it were to have been comprehensible when originally told the story must have had a recognisable basis in historical reality. This being so, it is of some significance that the master's first order, before his act of forgiveness, had been that the slave, his wife and children (and property) be sold to make good the debt [5].

Legal sources show that offspring from slave women was anticipated as a matter of course. References to female slaves and any issue they may have are common in the *Digest* and other major codes, as well as the more localised *Gnomon of the Idiologus* from Roman Egypt [6]. For its suggestiveness one legal ruling can again be noted particularly : in the early fourth century the emperor Constantine imposed a ban on the compulsory separation of slave families in Sardinia as a result of land redistribution, and ordered the reuniting of families already broken up in this way [7].

From evidence of this sort, spread over different times and places, it cannot be doubted that slave families existed in the Roman world, or that there was anything unusual about the fact. And epigraphic material simply confirms this view. Among the great mass of sepulchral inscriptions which have survived from the imperial age, many commemorate a deceased spouse and in so doing use formulaic expressions of the surviving partner's feelings. A bereaved husband would record that he had lived with his wife for a certain number of years 'without any complaint' and the partner would be spoken of in endearing terms [8]. The phraseology was doubtless highly conventional, much like its modern counterpart, but it suggests all the same a view of marriage based at least in part on mutual feelings of love, intimacy and respect [9]. Moreover, the inscriptions refer to marriages which were terminated not

---

(5) *Matt.* 18.23-34 ; cf. VOGT (1975), 142, for the essential statement that δοῦλος in the Gospels means 'slave'.

(6) E.g. *Dig.* 33.7.12.7 ; 27.1 ; *Instit.* 2.20.7 ; 16 ; *Gnom. Id.* 61. E. J. JONKERS, *Economische en sociale Toestanden in het romeinsche Rijk*, Wageningen, 1933, 113, gives a long list of legal texts which refer to *partus ancillarum* ; cf. also TREGGIARI (1979b), 194ff.

(7) *CTh.* 2.25.1 ; *CJ* 3.38.11 ; see also *Dig.* 33.7.27.1 (Africa) and cf. FINLEY (1980), 76.

(8) For formulae and examples of terms of endearment see Richmond LATTIMORE, *Themes in Greek and Latin Epitaphs*, Urbana, 1962, 277ff.

(9) For a more cautious view see HOPKINS (1965) ; contrast HOPKINS (1980), 325. Cf. in general Richard I. FRANK, *Augustus' Legislation on Marriage and Children* in *CSCA* 8 (1975) 41ff. ; BRUNT (1971), 558ff. ; FLORY (1978), 83ff.

by divorce or some other personal factor, but only by the death of one of the partners. All in all, the implication is strong that marriage was often regarded, once entered upon, as a binding and permanent union until the intervention of death ([10]).

It is not always possible to identify with absolute certainty the social status of the individuals mentioned in this great wealth of inscriptions, whether freeborn, freed or slave. But it is generally understood that all three categories are included in the material as a whole ([11]) ; marriages, that is, between slaves, or between persons who were slaves when their marriages began (they may have been subsequently set free), are definitely commemorated. What is important in such cases is that the phraseology and terms of endearment used are exactly the same as for persons of totally non-servile status, and not only the terms of affection but also the designative terms of reference such as *coniunx* (spouse) and, though less commonly, *uxor* (wife) and *maritus* (husband) as well ([12]), despite the fact that they were strictly inappropriate. Whatever the precise degree of romantic intimacy involved in marriages among the lower orders in Roman society, the evidence of the epitaphs suggests that servile attitudes towards marriage did not differ appreciably from those of the rest of society, that relationships were entered upon which slaves probably regarded as permanent arrangements, that such relationships endured over time, and that married slaves thought of each other as 'husband' and 'wife'. From marriages children followed, and the epitaphs show that slaves referred to one another as mother and father, son and daughter, brother and sister ([13]), again just as free members of society did. There is

---

(10) For the significance of women being married only once see WILLIAMS (1958) ; Marjorie LIGHTMAN and William ZEISEL, *'Univira'. An Example of Continuity and Change in Roman Society* in *Church History* 46 (1977), 19ff.

(11) For identification of slaves in inscriptions see the nomenclature principles outlined in WEAVER (1972), 42ff. and TREGGIARI (1975b), 393ff.

(12) E.g., *ILS* 7393 ; 7402 ; 7423 ; *CIL* 8.20084 ; etc. ; cf. ROULAND (1977), 264ff. ; TREGGIARI (1979b), 195. Presumably slaves who married marked their unions by some kind of marriage ceremony, but this is only a guess. PLAUT. *Cas.* 68, *seruiles nuptiae*, is suggestive but difficult to interpret ; the phrase could mean that ceremonies were common, or that the very idea of such was preposterous ; see generally J.-H. MICHEL, *Le Prologue de la "Casina" et le mariage d'esclaves* in *Hommages à Léon Hermann, Collection Latomus* 44, Brussels, 1960, 553ff. But note the expectation that Olympio and Casina will have children if married (*Cas.* 256 ; 291). The precision with which the duration of slave marriages was commemorated at least indicates that the wedding day was significant.

(13) E.g. *ILS* 7379 ; 7384 ; 7401 ; 7431 ; etc.

thus no cause to doubt that in the slave consciousness the family was anything but a perfectly natural and normal concept. The extent to which slave families existed at any one time or in any one place cannot be measured precisely, but the impression that the slave family was a common phenomenon is incontrovertible [14].

However, because slaves were technically not permitted to marry and could thus not produce legally recognisable families, the relationships which are attested in the sources must be considered concessions to slaves from their owners : it cannot be imagined, in light of owners' omnipotence over their slaves, that servile marriages occurred and lasted, or that children were born to married slaves, without the connivance if not express permission of masters [15]. In turn this implies that owners benefited from condoning servile familial relationships, a view which can be corroborated in principle from certain passages in Varro and Columella which suggest that Roman slave-owners encouraged slave families because their interests in preserving social and economic order were thereby served. First Varro :

> As to the breeding of herdsmen ; it is a simple matter in the case of those who stay all the time on the farm, as they have a female fellow-slave in the steading, and the Venus of herdsmen looks no farther than this. But in the case of those who tend the herds in mountain valleys and wooded lands, and keep off the rains not by the roof of the steading but by makeshift huts, many have thought that it was advisable to send along women to follow the herds, prepare food for the herdsmen, *and make them more diligent. (RR.* 2.10.6, Loeb translation).

Varro assumes here, and perhaps approvingly, that mating between and reproduction by slaves will occur spontaneously and he offers what appears to be a common view of slave-owners on the need to supply females to slave *pastores* on the trail not just for the practical purpose of preparing their food but to 'make them more diligent' (*assiduiores*)

(14) Cf. Finley (1976), 820. Veyne (1978), believes that between the end of the Republic and the Antonine age a moral transformation occurred as part of which marriage and the concept of conjugal love became more characteristic of Roman society than in earlier ages. If true this might mean that the importance of the family to slaves increased in the period of concern here. But Veyne's reluctance to present much evidence means that his hypothesis is difficult to evaluate. It seems, however, that the slave family was not a discovery of the Principate, and it is doubtful that Columella can be used to support the view that agricultural slaves of the first century lived in promiscuity.

(15) Cf. similarly Finley (1980), 75.

also ([16]). The same assumption of spontaneous sexual relationships among slaves appears in that passage from Columella in which he makes recommendations on the treatment of slaves drawn from his own experience :

> To women, too, who are unusually prolific, *and who ought to be rewarded* for the bearing of a certain number of offspring, I have granted exemption from work and sometimes even freedom after they had reared many children. For to a mother of three sons exemption from work was granted ; to a mother of more her freedom as well. (*RR*. 1.8.19, Loeb translation).

Both authors speak of the farm bailiff (*praefectus, uilicus*) and his family :

> The foremen are to be *made more zealous by rewards*, and care must be taken that they have a bit of property of their own, and mates from among their fellow-slaves to bear them children. (Varro, *RR*. 1.17.5, Loeb translation). But be the overseer what he may, he should be given a woman companion *to keep him within bounds* and yet in certain matters to be a help to him. (Col. *RR*. 1.8.5, Loeb translation).

Moreover, the passage from Tertullian already referred to ([17]), in which a connection is made between slaves marrying within the same household and order (*disciplina*), indicates that it was not the agricultural writers alone who understood the value of allowing slaves at least a semblance of family life.

It seems clear, then, that in many circumstances it was considered normal for slave families to exist, that the attitudes of slaves towards family life did not differ in essence from those of other sections of society, and that Roman slave-owners recognised the principle that permitting marital and familial associations among their slaves could contribute positively to the preservation of social and economic order. What now needs to be explored is the extent of familial stability in their lives that slaves might expect. How secure, in fact, were the relationships which they created ? The question is important because in everyday reality several factors arising from the ordinary practices of slave-owning acted

(16) Cf. also VARRO, *RR*. 2.1.26, *quod in hibernis habent in uillis mulieres, quidam etiam in aestiuis, et id pertinere putant, quo facilius ad greges pastores retineant, et puerperio familiam faciunt maiorem et rem pecuariam fructuosiorem.*

(17) *Ad ux.* 2.8.1, *Nonne etiam penes nationes seuerissimi quique domini et disciplinae tenacissimi seruis suis foras nubere interdicunt. Scilicet ne in lasciuiam excedant, officia deserant, dominica extraneis promant.* See Appendix C for remarks on Cato's attitude.

against the maintenance of familial stability and adversely affected the quality of servile life, yet such factors have hardly been taken into consideration in earlier estimates of slaves' family conditions [18]. Nonetheless, it must be emphasised that slaves were basically a form of property, and as commodities they were hence disposable. Slaves could be sold by one person to another, or left as part of a legacy without any obligation on the owner's part to take into account his slaves' domestic relationships. The arrangement of a marriage in free society might involve movement of slaves who were included in a dowry [19]. Slaves could even be loaned by one person to another, or given away as gifts as when the historian Appian sent two slaves to Fronto, the confidant of Marcus Aurelius [20]. Martial is found apparently seeking a slave from a patron for sexual reasons as if this were quite common [21]. The mechanics of the slave-owning system thus involved forcible transference of slaves from place to place and from owner to owner, and since slaves themselves had no control over such transference it was at times inevitable that their family conditions and arrangements be endangered. Some of these factors can be examined in detail.

The ability to be sold was the slave's most compelling reminder of his status as a sheer commodity, a point to be stressed since the frequent allusions to sales of slaves in the literary sources encourage a certain disregard of the dehumanising nature involved in the process of human exchange [22]. Turnover of slaves appears always to have been brisk, even in the later imperial age to judge from the schedule of slave prices contained in Diocletian's Edict on Maximum Prices of 301 [23]. But particularly rich information on sales is available from Roman Egypt in the form of records of actual transactions and this material is worth

---

(18) For generally favourable and optimistic views of servile family life see WESTERMANN (1955), 119 ; BIEZUNSKÁ-MAŁOWIST (1969), 95 ; BURFORD (1972), 51 ; BIEZUNSKÁ-MALOWIST (1973a), 88. The views of RAWSON (1966), 71ff., are more realistic : from the sepulchral evidence of Rome, she suggests common separation of slave children from their parents, at early ages ; it is not necessary, however, to believe that the parents of such children were engaged only in transitory unions. See also FLORY (1978), 88f.

(19) *P. Oxy.* 265 ; 496 ; APUL. *Apol.* 92 ; cf. PLAUT. *Asin.* 86.

(20) MART. *Epig.* 2.32 ; 8.52 ; FRONTO 1.264-9 (Haines, LCL).

(21) MART. *Epig.* 8.73. For the violent theft of a slave from her owner, see *P. Oxy.* 1120.

(22) On this aspect see further below, pp. 115ff.

(23) J. M. REYNOLDS, M. CRAWFORD, *The Aezani Copy of the Prices Edict* in ZPE 34 (1979), 163ff. at pp. 177 ; 198.

careful attention ([24]). The papyrological evidence from Egypt on slave sales extends from the first to the early fourth century, so that its seeming abundance is offset by its diffusion over time. But the legal framework of the relevant documents is fairly standardised throughout, and this allows some general observations to be made. First, the overwhelming majority of attested sales concern individual slave transactions, a fact long since recognised but the social significance of which has not been properly brought out. Of the few multiple transactions, most deal with sales of mothers and young children. Secondly, perhaps the most surprising fact which emerges is that the Egyptian evidence offers no example at all of the sale together of a husband and wife, or of a husband, wife and children. So on the assumption that the extant papyri are representative of the typical patterns of slave sales in Roman Egypt, it seems on statistical grounds alone that slave-owners were not affected when they sold slaves by any interest in preserving whatever familial ties their slaves had formed, with one or two exceptions ([25]). Given this predominant pattern of individual sales and the absence in the documentation of any full family group, it must follow that in all recorded instances there was a strong possibility of family disruption among slaves when they were sold.

Consideration of the ages at which slaves were sold substantiates these views. In Table I some recorded ages at which female slaves were sold are listed ([26]). The span ranges from a minimum of age four to a maximum of age thirty-five with a fairly even distribution in between. If children are separated from adult women, the dividing line occurring at age fourteen ([27]), the range of ages at which the latter were sold is that when

---

(24) The following remarks are developed from K. R. Bradley, *The Age at Time of Female Slaves* in *Arethusa* 11 (1978), 243ff. ; see also Andrew K. Dalby, *On Female Slaves in Roman Egypt* and K. R. Bradley, *Response* in *Arethusa* 12 (1979), 255ff. For transactions see Tables I and II.

(25) E.g. *P. Oxy.* 375 ; 1209.

(26) The sales records which supply ages constitute only a proportion of a longer catalogue of similar transactions where ages are not given. For full information see O. Montevecchi, *Ricerche di sociologia nei documenti dell'Egitto greco-romano : I contratti di compravendità* in *Aegyptus* 19 (1935), 11ff. ; Johnson (1936), 279ff. ; Oates (1969) ; Straus (1971) ; Montevecchi (1973), 211f. ; Biezunská-Małowist (1975).

(27) Age fourteen is chosen because literary evidence suggests that menarche in antiquity was believed to begin in the fourteenth year ; see Darrel W. Amundsen and Carrol Jean Diers, *The Age of Menarche in Classical Greece and Rome* in *Human Biology* 41 (1969), 125ff. ; cf. Hopkins (1965), 310ff. Although that age may seem low, it is supported by direct evidence of teenage motherhood in Egypt ; see, for example, *P. Oxy.* 1638, a female slave aged about twenty-five having a daughter aged about ten ; *P. Brux.* E

TABLE I*

No.	Date	Age at Sale	Remarks	Source
1	18/19-44/45	4		*BGU* 864 (987)
2	c.30	6		*P. Mich.* 278-9
3	108/116	7 (?)		*P. Strass.* 505
4	77	8		*P. Oxy.* 263
5	207	11	Pamphylian slave probably bought outside of Egypt	*P. Mich.* 546
6	180/192	13	Pontic slave	*SB* 9145
7	268/270	13		*SPP* XX 71
8	225	14		*P. Vindob. Bos.* 7
9	89	14	Fractional sale	*P. Oxy.* 332
10	3rd century	15	Libyan slave	*P. Ross.-Georg.* III 27
11	143	15	Fractional sale	*SB* 6291
12	252	17	Osrhoenian slave bought outside of Egypt	*P. Oxy.* 3043
13	37	17		*P. Mich.* 264-5
14	late 1st c.	18		*P. Lugd. Bat.* XIII 23
15	1st/2nd c.	18		*P. Oxy.* 1648
16	206	20	Lycian slave probably bought outside of Egypt	*BGU* 913
17	c.300	20		*SB* 8007
18	293	20	Cretan slave	*P. Lips.* 4-5
19	251/3	21	Slave sold with infant	*P. Oxy.* 1209
20	215	24	Asiatic slave	*P. Oxy.* 1463
21	138	24		*BGU* 805
22	early 2nd c.	24		*BGU* 2111
23	49	25		*P. Oxy.* 2582
24	234	25		*PSI* 182
25	129	25		*P. Oxy.* 95
26	late 1st c.	27	Fractional sale	*P. Lugd. Bat.* XIII 23
27	79	30		*P. Oxy.* 380
28	1st century	32		*P. Mich.* 281
29	Augustan	35		*BGU* 1059
30	1st century	35	Slave sold with two children	*P. Oxy.* 375

   * Not included here are the slave girl in Oates, (1969), whose age was below 19 ; and the infant in *PSI* 1228, whose age is given in Straus (1973), no. 25 as c. 2.

females reached the peak of their physical maturity. This is hardly surprising and would indeed be logical, since a prospective buyer would presumably be concerned above all with his purchase's capacity to undertake the work he needed to be done ([28]). Additionally, however, it should be noted that in the age span of fourteen to thirty-five female reproduction could most be expected ([29]), and given ancient views on the accidence of menopause ([30]) there is no example on record of a female slave being sold who might not have been expected to bear children after sale. A correlation thus seems indicated between the age of adult female slaves at time of sale and the period of expected reproductivity. If true, this can hardly be accidental, and it is generally agreed that one of the principal means of maintaining the servile population in the imperial age was through the breeding of slaves ([31]). To what extent slave-owners were able to breed new slaves systematically, if at all, is a question which cannot be definitively answered, yet the indications from Egypt are that reproduction by slaves was encouraged at least ([32]). And the present data suggest that female slaves may have been bought and sold with their potential for breeding acting as a prime consideration for buyers and sellers, which means in turn that economically the traffic in female slaves was not motivated solely by the slave's labour potential. Naturally the

7360, a free female aged about twenty-six having three children by a slave father, of whom the oldest is eight. Moreover, the common appearance in documents of the provision that any children born to a female slave after sale are to belong to her purchaser (see TAUBENSCHLAG (1955), 76), can be taken as a sign of biological maturity, or virtually so. For the appearance of the provision in a document referring to a fourteen year old, see *P. Vindob. Boswinkel* 7. The two thirteen year olds in Table I might still qualify as adults since no single age for menarche will apply in every instance. The high prices of these two slaves should be noted, as also the provision concerning future offspring in *SPP* XX 71.

(28) For occupations performed by female slaves in Egypt see STRAUS (1977); BIEZUNSKÁ-MAŁOWIST (1977), 73ff.

(29) The average age of slave women giving birth in Egypt has been computed to be 23 years and 45 days; see M. HOMBERT and C. PRÉAUX, *Recherches sur le recensement dans l'Egypte romaine* (*Pap. Lugd. Bat.* V, 1952), 171.

(30) Menopause in antiquity was thought to have occurred on average between ages forty and fifty; see Darrel W. AMUNDSEN and Carrol Jean DIERS, *The Age of Menopause in Classical Greece and Rome* in *Human Biology* 42 (1970), 79ff. For some examples of childbearing by women in their thirties see BIEZUNSKÁ-MAŁOWIST (1977), 113f.

(31) E.g. GSELL (1932), 398; WESTERMANN (1955), 84ff.; JONES (1968), 12; I. M. BIEZUNSKÁ-MAŁOWIST and M. MAŁOWIST, *La Procréation des esclaves comme source de l'esclavage* in *Mélanges offerts à K. Michalowski*, Warsaw, 1966, 275ff.; BRUNT (1971), 708; R. MEIGGS, *Roman Ostia²*, Oxford, 1973, 225.

(32) BIEZUNSKÁ-MAŁOWIST (1977), 113ff. See further below.

slave's capacity to reproduce cannot have been the only reason for the imposition of an upper age limit for the purchase of slaves, because if an earlier average age of death in antiquity than in the modern world can be assumed, the older the slave when acquired the greater the chance of a quickly diminishing return on the price invested in the property by the purchaser. Nevertheless, the reproduction factor was there.

The documentary evidence on slave sales does nothing to show how frequently they took place ; the impression simply remains that sale was common. The ability of females to provide their owners with new slaves may imply that at times the chances of establishing a stable family unit were good. But from the servile point of view the conclusion seems inescapable that any female slave could reasonably expect to be sold during her childbearing years because it was then that she was of greatest economic value to buyers and sellers alike, when interest in producing new slaves as well as the need for labour or capital were making themselves felt among owners. Presumably that expectation might have diminished as the slave advanced in years, but it must always have formed part of the female slave psychology ([33]).

The Egyptian evidence on ages of male slaves at time of sale as listed in Table II extends from a very young age of two years up to forty years with few examples of men being sold over the age of thirty. As is to be expected, adult males were again bought and sold in their prime, between ages fourteen and forty, and it is hardly likely that slaves over thirty had a great life expectancy left to them, probably few reaching what seems from one document to have been the 'retirement' age of sixty ([34]). Any purchase of a slave represented a considerable financial investment on the part of the buyer and, as with the females, return on the investment obviously diminished in proportion to the age of the slave when acquired. It might be believed, therefore, that slaves in the age span twenty-five to thirty, both men and women, could expect to go through their final transference as a result of sale and that their prospects of some years of relative familial stability increased about this time in their lives. This is not to say,

(33) What is envisaged is a situation where one owner no longer needed fertile women and was prepared to sell to another who did in return for hard cash. It can be noted that the ages of adult females when sold are comparable to those when free women might expect marriage to disrupt their lives. But that does not affect the rigours of disruption experienced by slaves.

(34) *P. Oxy.* 1030. For fourteen as the age of male majority and tax liability see JOHNSON (1936), 245 ; 248 ; and on life expectancy see references given below, p. 96 n. 53.

however, that such prospects were immune from the disruptive effects of other factors over which, as with sale, slaves had no control, and again the possibility of sale itself beforehand must have influenced men as well as women.

TABLE II

No.	Date	Age at Sale	Remarks	Source
1	c. 30	2	Sold with 6 yr. old girl	P. Mich. 278-9
2	1st/2nd c.	3		BGU 859
3	1st/2nd c.	3	See no. 4	P. Oxy. 1648
4	1st/2nd c.	4		P. Oxy. 1648
5	166	7	Mesopotamian slave	P. Lond. 229
6	136	8		BGU 193
7	143	8	Sold with 15 yr. old female	SB 6291
8	237	8	Macedonian slave	PSI 1254
9	116	8		SB 7573
10	250	13	Pontic slave	BGU 937
11	359	14	Gallic slave	BGU 316
12	154	17		SB 7555
13	212?	19		P. Oxy. 2777
14	198	19		P. Antin. 187
15		25		SB 7533
16	83	30	Sold with 40 yr. old male	P. Oxy. 94
17	late 1st c.	30		P. Oxy. 327
18	186	30		P. Oxy. 716
19	91/2	32		P. Oxy. 2856
20	91/2	38		P. Hamb. 63
21	83	40	Sold with 30 yr. old male	P. Oxy. 94

Familial disruption through sale is further implied by the evidence of sales of children who when sold were not accompanied by an adult. The material collected in Tables I and II implies that for sale children were compulsorily separated from their parents (and siblings) ; even the sale of children with mothers implies separation from fathers. It is possible of course that such separation had already taken place beforehand, following exposure as infants (^{35}) or previous transference of the children's parents, but in such cases as these sale might now mean severance from familiar surroundings and whatever surrogate attachments had been formed in a new household in the interim (^{36}).

Although children could and did work (^{37}), they obviously cannot have been as productive as adults because of their physical immaturity, and at first sight the traffic in slave children seems consequently odd. One explanation of the practice is that the low cost to the owner of maintaining a child after purchase, even over a period of years, was financially more attractive than the expenditure of a much larger capital sum for the acquisition later on of an adult slave (^{38}). But it might also be the case that children were bought for short-term speculative advantage as well as for long-term investment reasons, for this seems indicated by the case of a fourteen year old girl, who, when sold at that age, had already been sold at least three times previously in her young life (^{39}). How typical this case was cannot be said, but it is not an isolated example (^{40}), and a process of

(35) On the prevalence of child exposure throughout the Roman empire see Harris (1980), 123 ; exposure, however, was not synonymous with infanticide, for one view of which see Engels (1980) ; contrast W. V. Harris, *The Theoretical Possibility of Extensive Infanticide in the Graeco-Roman World* in *CQ* 32 (1982), 114ff.

(36) Cf. Watson (1968), 291ff. on the separation of slave mothers and children which resulted from Republican legal rulings on usufruct. When slaves were sold only locally they may have been allowed or secured access themselves to family members elsewhere, but the extent of this is hard to judge (see further below). This is true too for cases of unions between slave women and free men (on which cf. Biezunská-Małowist (1977), 115f.) where paternity of children was not acknowledged. For the sense of community engendered among slaves by their households see in general Flory (1978). A newly published papyrus, *P. Turner* (= *Papyri Greek and Roman... in Honour of Eric Gardner Turner*, London, 1981) 22, records the individual sale of a ten year old girl from Galatia at Side in Pamphylia in 142.

(37) For slave children working at early ages see Biezunská-Małowist (1969), and (1973a). For children in farming, Varro, *RR*. 2.10.1 ; 2.10.3 ; 3.5.15 ; 3.17.6 ; Col. *RR*. 8.2.7 ; 11.2.44.

(38) Biezunská-Małowist (1969), 96 ; (1973a), 84. The cost of 20dr. given by Diodorus Siculus (1.80.6) for the maintenance of a child until adulthood is of no value. In *BGU* 859 a man buys a three year old boy whose mother he had purchased two and a half years earlier ; the baby actually stayed with his mother, so the buyer deducted 200 dr. from the purchase price of 300 dr. as expenses for having previously supported the child.

(39) *P. Vindob. Boswinkel* 7, dated 225. There is some obscurity over the exact number of earlier sales ; cf. Biezunská-Małowist (1977), 39f.

(40) Cf. *P. Mich.* 546 where an eleven year old girl is being sold for probably the second time ; *P. Oxy.* 3054 where a male slave is being sold for the fourth time, though his age is unfortunately missing. The girl probably came from Paphlagonia ; Straus (1971), 363ff.

frequent exchange would of course have greatly intensified the degree of social disruption in slave children's lives.

The possibility of being sold away from family members always then threatened to disturb the personal lives of slaves. But that disturbance must have been exacerbated further by the distance involved in the transfer of the slave property. The papyrological evidence from Egypt illustrates the forced geographical mobility to which some slaves were exposed, and from this the potential for deracination in the lives of all slaves can be better understood. Many of the sales recorded in Roman Egypt appear to have concerned local transactions only, so that separated slaves may have found it possible to visit each other if owners agreed and vast distances did not have to be covered to do so. At Oxyrhynchus, which naturally supplies a large amount of information, the buyer and seller of a slave often both belonged to the town, and in such a small community it may not have been unduly difficult for slaves to contact one another, whether or not with the owners' permission. But while even this circumstance should not be taken to minimise the effects on family life that separation entailed, there remain nevertheless graphic examples of sales where transfer over substantial distances was, or had been, necessitated by one or a succession of transactions, especially so in cases where a slave in Egypt had been imported from outside the country. In order to demonstrate a process constantly at work throughout the imperial period, the following cases can be particularly noted.

In 49 a twenty-five year old woman named Demetrous, a homeborn slave from the village of Taamechis in the Heracleopolite nome, was purchased by a woman from Oxyrhynchus. In 129 another woman, Dioscorous, also aged twenty-five, was bought by a resident of Oxyrhynchus from a man who had earlier bought the woman from an Alexandrian citizen. Sotas, an eight year old boy, was sold in 136 by a woman from Ptolemais Euergetis to another woman whose husband was also a citizen of Alexandria. In 151 a Phrygian slave named Sambatis was sold to an Alexandrian, the transaction occurring at Side in Pamphylia. In 215 a woman from Oxyrhynchus wished to purchase a twenty-four year old female slave named Tyrannis from the present owner who lived at Choinothis in the Heracleopolite nome ; if the sale were concluded, movement to Oxyrhynchus would not have been the first dislocation in the slave's life, since she was of Asiatic origin. A thirteen year old boy, Karos, was sold in 250 at Heracleopolis Magna, the home of both buyer and seller ; although no great distance could have been involved in this transfer, the boy had somehow come to Egypt from Pontus. In 252 a seventeen year old female, Balsamea, who appears to have been born in Osrhoene, had arrived by unknown circumstances at Tripolis in Phoenicia, where she was sold to a man from Oxyrhynchus who took her back and locally registered his purchase. Also in the mid-third century the purchase of a male slave named Prokopton was registered at Oxyrhynchus, the sale having taken place at Bostra in Arabia where Prokopton had already had three previous owners in succession, in the house of the first of whom he had been born. In 267 a female slave named Nike passed from the ownership of one soldier to another, the exchange occurring in Alexandria although the woman was Arabian in origin. Finally, from a document which eventually found its way to Hermopolis there is the example from 293 of a twenty year old female slave originally from Crete who was sold to a man from Antinoopolis by a citizen of Alexandria ([41]).

In cases such as these it is not possible to tell how many of the slaves had started life as exposed infants and had lost their parents this way. But when transfer over considerable distances occurred, there can have been little hope of slaves maintaining contact with their places of birth or earlier residence where personal relationships might have been formed. The examples which have been cited all concern individual sales only, so there is no likelihood that adult women were kept with any children born to them before sale. A homeborn slave in Egypt had a certain advantage in knowing that sale out of the country was unlikely (it was illegal) ([42]), but being homeborn was no protection in and of itself against the threat of sale and movement within Egypt. Apart from the evidence of the sales of mothers and children together, no more than a handful of the full number of recorded sales, it seems that slave-owners were little troubled about breaking servile familial ties when economic considerations made sale of their slaves attractive or necessary.

---

(41) The examples in this paragraph are respectively from *P. Oxy.* 2582 ; *P. Oxy.* 95 ; *BGU* 193 ; *P. Oxy.* 1463 ; *BGU* 937 ; *P. Oxy.* 3053 ; *P. Oxy.* 3054 ; *P. Oxy.* 2951 ; *P. Lips.* 4 and 5. For background see STRAUS (1971); BIEZUNSKÁ-MAŁOWIST (1975), and on Oxyrhynchus in particular see E. G. TURNER, *Roman Oxyrhynchus* in *JEA* 38 (1952), 78ff. ; *Oxyrhynchus and Rome* in *HSCP* 79 (1975), 1ff.

(42) Export of slaves from Egypt was controlled, as known from *Gnom. Id.* 65-67 ; but sections 67 and 69 suggest that despite the law exports did sometimes take place. Egyptian slaves in other parts of the Roman world are known.

The documentary evidence on slave sales in other parts of the Roman world is far less copious than for Egypt, but it cannot be doubted that the generally negative picture for the stability of servile familial arrangements which the Egyptian records give was not applicable elsewhere as well. A small number of (individual) sales documents from Dacia belonging to the second century include the exchange of a six year old girl named Passia, of a Cretan woman named Theudote, and of a Greek boy, Apalaustus [43]. From Dura-Europus there are records of the sale of a twenty year old male between two brothers in 180 and of a twenty-eight year old woman in 243 [44]. And an exchange of a seven year old boy named Abbas (Eutyches) in Syria in 166 is also known [45]. None of this material is at odds with the evidence from Egypt. Moreover, the existence of a substantial body of Roman law governing sales of slaves [46] and the frequent allusions to sales and slave-dealers in the literature of the imperial age [47] are strongly suggestive of a brisk turn-over among owners, of slaves suffering separation from kin, and of considerable distances being covered as a result of sale. The younger Pliny, for instance, is found

---

(43) *FIRA*[2] III no. 87 (139): no. 89 (160); no. 88 (142).

(44) *P. Dura* 25; 28.

(45) *FIRA*[2] III no. 132. Cf. VEYNE (1961), 215 for the presumption of common sale of children throughout the Empire, and note the accounts of L. Caecilius Iucundus from Pompeii in FRANK (1940), 255. In PLAUT. *Merc.*, the plot involves purchase of a slave girl in Rhodes who is transported to Athens to be sold again. Despite the fiction, the circumstances of compulsory movement and frequent change of ownership (in this case a two year interval is involved; cf. 534-7) are the same as shown above from the documentary sources. The geography of the slave trade outside Egypt is much illuminated by HARRIS (1980), 125ff., who clearly demonstrates as well considerable movement of slaves from one region of the empire to another.

(46) For the law see BUCKLAND (1908), 39ff. The following extract from the Edict of the Curule Aediles (c. 129) is representative: 'Whoever sells slaves shall inform the buyers what sickness or defect each slave has, who is a runaway or a vagabond or is not free from noxal liability; and when they sell the said slaves they shall announce openly and correctly all the said points. If any slave is sold contrary to these regulations or if whatever the buyer alleges must be properly performed in this regard is contrary to the statement or the promise made when he was being sold: we shall grant an action to him and to all persons to whom the matter pertains in six months from the time when first there is an opportunity to try the matter by law, that this slave may be returned'. Translation from A. C. JOHNSON, P. R. COLEMAN-NORTON, F. C. BOURNE, *The Corpus of Roman Law (Corpus Iuris Romani), Volume II, Ancient Roman Statues*, Austin, 1961, no. 245. Cf. also D. DAUBE, *Forms of Roman Legislation*, Oxford, 1956, 92ff.

(47) On slave-dealers see HARRIS (1980) and below, pp. 114ff. For incidental slave sale references, see HOR. *Epist.* 2.2.1-19; SEN. *Epp.* 80.9; IUV. 6.373; 11.147; QUINT. *Inst.* 2.15.25; APUL. *Apol.* 45; 92; 93; GELL. *NA* 6.4; 4.2.1.

buying slaves, anxious only about their reliability [48]. The elder Pliny tells of the infamous dealer Toranius who, for a good price, sold two slave boys to the triumvir M. Antonius as twins, despite the fact that one came from Asia and the other from Gaul [49]. The story has an amusing aspect, but it also hints at the harshness of separation more directly visible in the case of a slave family owned by Juvenal. The poet speaks of a boy in domestic service at Rome who had been taken from his parents on Juvenal's farm at Tibur, apparently to the boy's great distress [50]. Even more vivid is the depiction on the funeral stele [51] of the slave-trader A. Kapreilius Timotheus from the Black Sea of a train of chained slaves being led away for disposal by sale, almost a photographic capture of what must have been a common sight in antiquity since slave-trading was ubiquitous throughout the Roman Empire [52]. A recent hypothesis has been advanced that the Roman government of the Augustan age expected some 250,000 sales of slaves among Roman citizens each year [53] and although the accuracy of the figure is hardly verifiable, it certainly conforms with impressions left by various kinds of evidence. As far as the sale of female slaves is concerned, nothing conflicts with what has been suggested on their attractiveness to purchasers as providers of future slaves, and an important item from the *Digest* may indeed be taken to confirm the high value of women in their childbearing years : it was a common legal opinion that pregnancy was no barrier to the sale of a woman, because reproduction was her greatest responsibility [54]. Breeding certainly took

(48) PLIN. *Epp.* 1.21.2.

(49) PLIN. *NH* 7.56.

(50) IUV. 11.146ff. ; cf. G. HIGHET, *Juvenal the Satirist*, Oxford, 1954, 131 ; 237. Observe the separation of a slave apprentice from his mother in TREGGIARI (1979b), 191.

(51) For which see J. ROGER, *Revue Archéologique*⁶ 24 (1945), 49ff. : *AE* 1946, no. 229. It should be noted that besides the eight chained slaves, the scene on the stele also includes two women and two children who are not in chains. Whether these people were also slaves and related to the men or the family of the dealer himself cannot be stated.

(52) HARRIS (1980), 126ff.

(53) HARRIS (1980), 121.

(54) *Dig.* 21.1.14.1, *Si mulier praegnas uenierit, inter omnes conuenit sanam eam esse : maximum enim ac praecipuum munus feminarum est accipere ac tueri conceptum.* This opinion appears to have superseded that given by VITRUVIUS (2.9.1) in the Augustan age. Cf. VEYNE (1978), 55. The objection might be made that since the importance of slavery in the economy of Egypt was substantially less than in that of Italy (slaves were barely used in Egyptian agriculture), the evidence of the Egyptian papyri is irrelevant for practices elsewhere in the empire. Yet if insistence is made on the point that slavery as a social institution is the main object of concern here, then the principles of the detailed Egyptian material are not at all irrelevant for other areas ; cf. above p. 17 n. 18. TREGGIARI (1979b),

place, and the results were highly prized ([55]).

A certain tension can thus be perceived between the fact that slaves married and produced children when conditions allowed and the fact that certain factors operated in their lives which were beyond their control. Although owners encouraged servile familial life when it was in their interests to do so, those narrow interests did not permit any deep concern for the human relationships their slaves formed to intervene in their thinking when sale was decided upon.

From Roman Egypt many examples have also survived of bequests of property ([56]) which sometimes included slaves, and this material can be used to add to knowledge of slaves' expectations. In general terms a low possibility for the retention of family connections upon transfer of this type arises from the point that in Egypt itself slave households tended to be small in comparison with the establishments of wealthy aristocrats at Rome ([57]). A document recently published suggests ownership of perhaps one hundred slaves by a single individual in Alexandria early in the second century ([58]), but such a large household would be very much an exception to the rule. Thus, if a slave-owner had several heirs and his property were divided at his death more or less equally among them, the chances had to be high that servile relationships would suffer as a result. It often happened that slaves were fractionally divided among heirs (and not just in Egypt but elsewhere too), a rather curious arrangement whose practical effects are not at all properly understood ([59]). Additionally, slaves

187f. comments on the attractiveness of female slaves for breeding purposes visible in legal sources on sale, but doubts, on the basis of *Dig.* 5.3.27 pr., that breeding was 'the *main* function of women slaves' (her emphasis, p. 188). Complementary functions, however, do not require primacy of one over the other, and it is only to be expected that owners who did purchase slaves with their breeding potential in mind would have exercised due caution beforehand, as the text from the *Digest* suggests.

(55) Cf. STAERMAN-TROFIMOVA (1975), 17f. ; TREGGIARI (1979b), 187ff. ; HARRIS (1980), 120f. ; FINLEY (1980), 130. 'Breeding' of slaves is a difficult term to define because the conscious element on the slave-owner's part in it could obviously not be the same as in the breeding of livestock on the farm. This problem is reflected in Varro who certainly speaks of *fetura humana pastorum* (*RR*. 2.10.6) and who can recommend the most suitable kind of women for *pastores* (*RR*. 2.10.7), but who is unable to devote the same amount of space to the topic as with animals.

(56) See generally BIEZUNSKÁ-MAŁOWIST (1977), 116ff. ; cf. MONTEVECCHI (1973), 207ff.

(57) See above, p. 16.

(58) *P. Oxy.* 3197 (see introduction to the text by J. D. Thomas) ; cf. BIEZUNSKÁ-MAŁOWIST (1977), 96f., who believes the household may have included more than a hundred slaves ; BIEZUNSKÁ-MAŁOWIST (1976).

(59) See in general I. M. BIEZUNSKÁ-MAŁOWIST, *Les Esclaves en copropriété dans*

could be and were sold off by the new owner to pay the testator's debts or burial expenses, or a surviving wife might be allowed to control a minor's inheritance until the latter's coming of age [60]. Provisions such as these were again likely to have an impact on the lives of the property being handled.

The complications that arose from the death of a slave-owner, as well as the lack of certain knowledge of how transmitted slaves subsequently fared, can be demonstrated by reference to a number of specific documents. First, in a papyrus from the late third century [61] property and land are divided between the two families of a deceased man who had been married twice during his lifetime. Seven children had been born to the two wives, respectively two and five, among whom four slaves were now equally apportioned (i.e. fractionally) in the father's will. Thus the children of the first family, a brother and sister, received two-sevenths of the four slaves, the remainder going to the other five children, three of whom were minors. What the de facto arrangements the heirs made were is not at all clear, but they may have been less confused than the formal situation suggests. If in actuality the three minors were too young to have had effective supervision of their share of the property, the solution may have been that two slaves went to the children of the first marriage (even though they did not have full legal title), while the two other slaves went to the two older children (brothers) of the second marriage. Three of the slaves' names are recorded in the papyrus and they include those of a twenty-five year old woman and her ten year old daughter ; it may have happened that mother and daughter were kept together under the new arrangements, but little more than the bare possibility can be stated.

A second document tells of a father who again bequeathed four slaves, this time to three sons [62]. Three of these slaves were female and apparently still of an age to reproduce. The two older sons each received one slave, respectively a man and a woman, while the youngest son was given two slaves ; of these, however, one was lame and the use of the

---

l'Egypte gréco-romaine in Aegyptus 48 (1968), 116ff. On the tendency to divide property equally, HOPKINS (1980), 322.

(60) P. Oxy. 493 ; P. Ryl. 153. For the element of uncertainty which affected slaves note also Instit. 2.20.22, Si generaliter seruus uel alia res legetur, electio legatarii est, nisi aliud testator dixerit.

(61) P. Oxy. 1638.

(62) P. Mich. 323-325 + PSI 903 = A. S. HUNT, C. C. EDGAR, Select Papyri I, LCL, 1932, no. 51 (47).

other was reserved for the former owner's wife. No provision for joint ownership was made, and it is not known whether the sons already had their own independent households or still all resided together. In either case it is difficult to see how the three female slaves could have reproduced, as seems expected [63], unless access were available to men other than the one member of the original household.

Even more perplexing on the question of sexual balance, or imbalance, among slaves is that document already mentioned [64], which lists a large number of slaves from one household who were divided equally among three sons after their father's death. Some forty-five slaves are named in the papyrus, but it appears that some of these were effectively owned by the sons while their father was still alive. All the slaves allotted, however, were men, which led the editor of the text to estimate a possible total number of one hundred slaves for the full establishment since females must have been included, and the text is not complete. One son already had possession of a female slave and two others are mentioned in order to differentiate their homonymous sons (Alexander son of Anabasis and Alexander son of Gemella). Further, the text speaks of other slaves, not listed, remaining the common property of the heirs, which might mean females. A total of one hundred slaves, however, would be an exceptionally large sized household for Roman Egypt, as already seen, and it may perhaps be doubted that the number of women equalled that of the men. No ages of the slaves are provided, so how many of the named males were children (presumably some were) cannot be known. The division among the three brothers was supposed to take place by lot, but it is worth noticing that one of the heirs received three slave brothers, one of whom was called Gemellus and so just possibly the brother of the Gemella who had a son Alexander. Alexander, himself, however, went to a different heir.

A third example which deserves attention is a document from the mid first century which is rather unusual in view of the detailed information it gives concerning the distribution of a slave household on the owner's death [65]. The text is by no means free from ambiguity but it allows for a tentative interpretation at least. The circumstances were that eighteen

---

(63) The clause concerning anticipated future offspring from females (above n. 27) appears in this document.

(64) *P. Oxy.* 3197 ; see n. 58 above.

(65) *P. Mich.* 326 ; cf. BIEZUNSKÁ-MAŁOWIST (1977), 119f.

slaves were divided among six heirs, brothers and sisters [66], five of whom had belonged to the children's father, the remaining thirteen to their mother [67]. The paternally owned slaves are as follows : Agathous, Herakles, Euphrosynon, Epaphras and Leontas. Of these Agathous was the mother of Herakles and Euphrosynon who were thus brother and sister [68]. The list of maternally owned slaves runs thus : Herakleia, Narkissos the barber, Sarapas, Euphrosynon, Nike, Thermouthis, Serapous, Euphrosynos, Helene, Thaubas, Ganymas, Athene, and Narkissos the muleteer. The document is clear that Herakleia had a certain number of children, who seem to extend in the list from Narkissos the barber to, and including, Serapous, that is a total of six, although Serapous might have to be excluded [69]. In turn, however, Serapous is described as the mother of the following Euphrosynos who may consequently have been Herakleia's grandchild. Helene definitely did not belong to the family of Herakleia because her mother was a certain Herous who already had been sold away from the household, unless she was related by marriage. But a three-generational slave family may nonetheless be in evidence here, comprising a mother, her six children and a grandson. Among the remaining slaves Thaubas was the mother of Ganymas and Athene. So from the total of eighteen slaves three families are partially represented at least, though fathers and husbands cannot be safely identified from the text as it stands. The following chart shows how the full complement of slaves was allocated to the heirs according to the terms of the division.

P. Mich. 326

Herakleides the elder	Maron	Herodes
Herakles*	Leontas	Agathous*
Serapous† +	Herakleia†	Euphrosynon I*
Euphrosynos +	Ganymas Ø	Epaphras
	Narkissos the muleteer	

(66) Their names were Herakleides the elder, Maron, Herodes, Didymus, Herakleides the younger, Herakleia.

(67) Clearly, however, the document is concerned with a united household.

(68) *P. Mich.* 326 line 7.

(69) *P. Mich.* 326 lines 8-9. The text makes the exact number of Herakleia's children uncertain : Ἡράκλειαν τὴν καὶ Τααρμιῦσιν καὶ ταύτης τέκνα Νάρκισσον κουρέα καὶ Σαραπᾶν καὶ Εὐφρόσυνον καὶ Νίκην καὶ Θερμοῦθιν καὶ Σεραποῦν καὶ ταύτης τέκνα Εὐφρόσυνον καὶ Ἑλένην ἔγγονον Ἡροῦτος ἐκ τῆς προπεπραμένης ἔτι πάλαι. Some scholars assume a break before καὶ Σεραποῦν, to give Herakleia only five children ; BIEZUNSKÁ-MAŁOWIST (1977), 119 ; HARRIS (1980), 135 n. 39. But this cannot be certain and a reading with no break is preferred here.

Didymus	Herakleides the younger	Herakleia
Euphrosynon II†	Thaubas Ø	Narkissos the barber†
Thermouthis†	Athene Ø	Nike†
	Sarapas†	Helene

Sigla denote certain and possible familial connections

Although the ascription of family ties is to a large extent tentative, it seems from the allocations that Thaubas and her daughter were kept together, but that Thaubas' other child Ganymas was separated from her ; that Agathous was kept with her child Euphrosynon, but that her other child Herakles was also separated from the mother ; that Herakleia was separated from all her children, though among the latter siblings remained together on two occasions, while Serapous and Euphrosynos also stayed together. Only Sarapas and Herakleia were not put with another family member, and in the newly formed groups only one contains no obvious continuation of a family tie of some sort.

Unfortunately the document gives no information on the ages of these slaves. If indeed Herakleia was a grandmother she must by ancient standards have been quite elderly, and the two men named Narkissos might be presumed to be adults since specific occupations are assigned to them. Many of the females must have been adult or close to adulthood either because they had already given birth to children (Agathous, Thaubas, Serapous) or because future offspring from them was anticipated (Nike, Thermouthis, Helene, Athene)[70]. Since Serapous was of childbearing age her siblings may have been close to adulthood or even older. Under the terms of the division Serapous may conceivably have been 'paired' with Herakles, Agathous with Epaphras, Helene with Narkissos the barber, Thaubas with Sarapas. But Athene, Thermouthis and Nike apparently had no access to men, unless the possibility of brother-sister couplings is brought into the picture [71].

Highly speculative as this reconstruction is, it may nonetheless give some slight indication that attention was given to the preservation of familial connections among slaves when they were divided up after their owners' deaths. Similarly, another document from the mid second century shows that of six slaves who were divided between two heirs (a

(70) Again the clause concerning future offspring is applied to these women (above n. 27).

(71) On which in general see Hopkins (1980).

brother and sister), a woman was kept with her two children on one hand and a second woman apparently set free retained custody of her ten-month old twins (still slaves) on the other [72]. But the extent of this concern should not be exaggerated. In the last example the twins were to return to their new owner six months after weaning, so that the original failure to separate mother and children appears to have had a practical purpose behind it, while with a family as large as that of Herakleia appears to have been it was virtually inevitable that some family connections be maintained in the division. Moreover, Serapous and her child might also have been kept together for practical reasons. It cannot be known whether the divided families had access to each other once the new groups had been formed, or whether these groups came to constitute totally distinct entities. Nor can it be known whether the six heirs already owned slaves other than those they now received who might have served as possible wives and husbands for the new batches. At most, therefore, concern was limited, and from the cases which have been presented the general impression prevails that interest in the disposal of property as property prevailed over sentiment or sympathy for the emotional wellbeing of the slaves who composed it.

Although the provisions of documents of the kind considered so far were often intricate enough, further complications could set in if the provisions were subsequently overturned, and it is clear that on occasions certain heirs did act contrary to the directions given in wills. The result was further difficulty for the slave. A papyrus from the late third century [73], for example, reveals the inability of a young woman to secure title to her apparent share of bequeathed slaves who were being held by two of the woman's uncles. An appeal was addressed to the governor of Egypt, but the outcome, and the fate of the slaves, is unknown. Again in the third century a claim of false ownership of slaves was brought by a man against his great-uncle's heirs : two children had been born to a slave woman owned by the petitioner's mother (now dead) and had been fraudulently claimed by the great-uncle ; although the mother had resecured ownership while alive, the heirs of the great-uncle, once he died, had again claimed the slaves, which led to the present appeal for redress [74]. The struggle was obviously one for property and nothing else.

(72) *P. Strass.* 122.
(73) *P. Oxy.* 2713.
(74) *P. Oxy.* 1468.

Finally, the case can be noted of a similar struggle in the early second century between two brothers on one hand against a third party on the other : the brothers claimed ownership of a female slave by virtue of inheritance, but obviously did not have such ownership. Once more the issue was so involved that the strategus of the nome referred it to the governor ([75]).

Once the papyrological material from Roman Egypt is set aside, there is virtually no other documentary evidence from elsewhere to show slaves being bequeathed to new owners, an indication of the paucity of surviving sources. Yet again it cannot be imagined that the problems and complexities which have been seen in the Egyptian material were unique to one part of the Roman world. Roman legal sources make clear that slaves were property which could be left by will to new owners and the application of Roman law was not of course confined to Italy alone ([76]). The well known will of Dasumius, belonging to 108, seems to show the process in operation at Rome itself of slaves being willed to heirs, though details are obscure because of the highly fragmentary nature of the text ([77]). In literary sources, however, incidental remarks provide confirmation, such as Varro's statement that inheritance gave full legal ownership of slaves, Petronius' reference to a chef who had been left by will to Trimalchio (to Trimalchio's ignorance), or Apuleius' statement that Pudentilla had made over to her sons some four hundred slaves ([78]), remarks which are of interest because of their ordinary nature. And an inscription from Rome is suggestive of the emotional upheaval which might be presumed in the lives of slaves when owners' wishes affected their relationships : a woman named Furia Spes, apparently a freedwoman, made a dedication to her deceased husband, L. Sempronius Firmus, apparently a freedman, in which she recorded that wife and husband had loved each other since childhood, had married, but then after a short interval had been involuntarily separated 'by an evil hand' ([79]). When

(75) *P. Oxy.* 97.
(76) See BUCKLAND (1908), 15ff. ; cf. BOYER (1965), 357f. ; 366 ; 370f. ; 387 ; 400 ; TREGGIARI (1979a), 69ff. ; (1979b), 196ff. Servile *agnomina* also indicate transference of slave property ; cf. WEAVER (1972), 212ff.
(77) *FIRA*² III no. 48.
(78) VARRO, *RR*. 2.10.4 ; PETR. *Sat.* 47.11-13 ; APUL. *Apol.* 93 ; cf. PLIN. *Epp.* 10.104-105, Pliny left as the patron of Junians.
(79) *ILS* 8006. The full circumstances of the couple are not clear, and *a manu mala diseparati sumus* may, however, mean separation by death.

property was left by one person to another with slaves on it, it may be that at times no changes occurred in the personal lives of the slaves concerned. But all in all the conclusion seems justified that the death of a slave-owner must have been a difficult time indeed for his slaves because the world which they had created for themselves was threatened with possible extinction ([80]). Anxiety about or fear of severance can never have been far from the minds of those slaves who had been able successfully to form family units.

The possibility of disruption following sale or bequest was a pressure to which all slave families were exposed. A further circumstance and constraint can now be outlined which must have had a more restricted application, but which was nonetheless important for those affected by it and which continues the theme of economic exploitation overpowering emotional concern. The evidence again in the first instance comes from papyri.

In contracts for the hire of wet-nurses, several of which still remain ([81]), the stipulation is commonly found that the nurse was not to sleep with a man or become pregnant during the period covered by the contract, an interval which ranged from a minimum of six months to a maximum of three years, with two years being that most frequently found ([82]). The

---

(80) It must be remembered here that slaves could be set free in their owners' wills (see below, pp. 97ff.), though manumission was not universal in this situation. Also, there should be no inference that all slave-owners all of the time were universally indifferent to their slaves' situations ; this cannot have been the case. But in light of what is detectable from the documentary papyri on sales and bequests the statement that the 'creation of a slave family... could not be ignored by masters with any degree of feeling' (WEAVER (1972), 191) may be considered questionable.

(81) Examples are collected in BRADLEY (1980), 321ff., from which the following remarks are derived and in which other secondary references are available ; cf. additionally BIEZUNSKÁ-MAŁOWIST (1977), 24ff. ; 104f. ; and for a new document see S. M. E. VAN LITH, *Lease of Sheep and Goats. Nursing Contract with Accompanying Receipt* in *ZPE* 14 (1974), 145ff.

(82) 'So long as she is duly paid she shall take proper care both of herself and of the child, not injuring her milk nor sleeping with a man nor becoming pregnant' ; *BGU* 1107, translated by A. S. HUNT, C. C. EDGAR, *Select Papyri* I, LCL, 1932 no. 16. See also *BGU* 1058 ; 1106 ; 1108 ; 1109 ; *SB* 7607 ; 7619, *P. Bour.* 14 ; *P. Ross.-Georg.* II 18 ; XVI ; LXXIV ; *ZPE* 14 (1974), 148. The following periods are specified as indicated : six months, *P. Meyer* 11 ; eight months, *BGU* 1110 ; ten months, *BGU* 1109 ; twelve months, *BGU* 1112 ; fifteen months, *BGU* 1108 ; sixteen months, *BGU* 1107 ; eighteen months, *BGU* 1106 ; two years, *BGU* 297 ; 1058 ; *SB* 7619 ; *PSI* 203 ; 1065 ; *P. Bour.* 14 ; *P. Oxy.* 37 and 38 ; 91 ; *P. Ross.-Georg.* II 18 ; LXXIV ; *ZPE* 14 (1974), 148ff. ; two years, six months, *SB* 7607 ; three years, *P. Tebt.* 399.

reason for this provision was a concern to protect the nurse's supply of milk for the nursling [83], a view supported by Soranus' recommendation of sexual abstinence for wet-nurses on both physical and emotional grounds :

> For coitus cools the affection toward < the > nursling by the diversion of sexual pleasure and moreover spoils and diminishes the milk or suppresses it entirely by stimulating menstrual catharsis through the uterus or by bringing about conception [84].

Under these conditions a great degree of self-control seems to have been required in the private lives of wet-nurses, even for the minimum contractual period known. Wet-nurses could be free or slave women, but distinctions of status did not affect the obligation to sexual abstinence to which they were bound [85]. Some of the attested free nurses were married [86], and the implication follows that while nursing normal marital arrangements had to be discontinued. While slave nurses could not of course have had legal marriages, it seems reasonable to imagine that for them too some personal relationships may well have been affected once a contract was entered upon, whether with a slave or free partner [87], since a wet-nurse must have given birth herself in order to fulfill her function. Quite obviously the degree to which such interruptions were experienced depended upon the extent to which the provision was maintained, a factor which cannot be measured. But the nursing contracts contained stringent penalty clauses against breach and in the case of slave nurses their owners were required to return any sums of money received for nursing services and to pay an additional fine as well [88]. The owners were concerned above all to exploit the potential of a labour force at their disposal and producing income lay behind the agreements that were made. This could give reason consequently for

---

(83) See for example *SB* 7619 : καὶ [μὴ] ἀνδροχοιτεῖν πρὸς τὸ μὴ διαφθαρῆναι [τὸ γάλα ...

(84) SORANUS, *Gynaecology* 2.19, translated by O. TEMKIN, *Soranus' Gynecology*, Baltimore, 1956.

(85) Slave nurses appear in *BGU* 1058 ; 1109 ; 1111 ; 1112 ; *PSI* 1065 ; *P. Oxy.* 91 ; *P. Tebt.* 399.

(86) See *BGU* 297 ; 1106 ; 1110 ; *SB* 7607 ; 7619 ; *PSI* 203 ; 1131 ; *P. Meyer* 11 ; *P. Ross.-Georg.* II 18 ; LXXIV ; *ZPE* 14 (1974), 149f. ; where the nurse's husband appears as *kyrios* in the contracts.

(87) For relationships between slave women and free men see BIEZUNSKA-MAŁOWIST (1969) ; (1977), 115f.

(88) See for example *BGU* 1107 ; 1109.

believing that in general the provisions of the contracts were not usually disregarded because the financial losses to be incurred were too great a liability and the nurses may also have feared punishment from their owners.

Broad assertions about private behaviour, however, are perhaps best avoided when they cannot be corroborated, especially since the relevant documents extend over a large span of time which may have provoked varying forms of response [89]. The possibilities, however, can be simply stated : the provision against sexual activity was either observed by slave wet-nurses or it was not. If it was, it follows that sexual continence formed a staple element in the life of the nurse and that at any moment in time a certain number of slave women were obliged to make some alteration in the normal marital situation which could be inferred, in some instances at least, from the birth of their own children. If it was not, then the danger of an unwanted pregnancy must have led to the use of some kind of birth control [90]. In either case a not inconsiderable burden was imposed on the slave women and their male partners. Moreover, because it was the decision of the nurse's owner, not of the nurse herself, which led to the restrictions suggested there was no element of choice for the woman involved here but rather one of compulsion. In consequence the nursing contracts, as far as slave wet-nurses are concerned, seem to provide some illustration of how in antiquity the owner's absolute authority extended into the most intimate areas of his slaves' lives and behaviour [91]. The economic basis of the employment of slave nurses, which has to do with the owner's development of resources at his disposal more than with anything else, led to the overriding of concern for the finer feelings of the nurses who were hired out.

Moreover, wet-nursing was probably a widespread occupation for women of low social status throughout the Roman world. Literary sources again suggest this, while for Rome itself a certain amount of epigraphic material is available to show nursing of infants of all social levels [92]. Further, if it is true to believe that the *columna lactaria* in the

---

(89) The nursing papyri, which include receipts for services as well as contracts for employment of nurses, extend from 15 B.C. (*BGU* 1111) to A.D. 305 (*P. Grenf.* 75).

(90) See further BRADLEY (1980), 323f.

(91) On the sexual abuse of slaves see further below, pp. 117f.

(92) Cf. DIO CHRYS. *Orat.* 7.14 ; GELL. *NA* 12.1 ; TAC. *Dial.* 28-29 ; for the epigraphic evidence see TREGGIARI (1976), 88f.

Forum Holitorium was so-called because infants were commonly brought there to be nursed ([93]), another indication of the common nature of the job emerges. It is plausible to believe, therefore, that the compulsive effect argued from the Egyptian evidence was experienced on a broad scale.

Up to this point certain factors which threatened interference in servile familial life have been illustrated from the relatively detailed evidence provided by Egyptian papyri and the probability of their application elsewhere, at least in principle, has been stated. The estimate of slaves' prospects for successful family life can next be taken further by considering in conjunction, and on a wider geographical scale, information on the nature of the households to which slaves belonged and on the balance of male to female slaves in different locations. One of the points to emerge from the Egyptian documents is that it is seldom apparent where slaves found partners who might become their husbands or wives since slave holdings were small and the availability of partners must often have been consequently restricted ([94]). A certain proportion of slave infants must always, without doubt, have been the product of casual relationships, voluntary or otherwise, between female slaves and the free members of their owners' households, relationships which can in general only have been an impediment to slave familial stability ([95]). But the question of access by slaves of one sex to another requires further comment.

In the great aristocratic households of Rome itself, where slaves numbered in the hundreds, women's availability to men was probably higher than in the rural areas of Italy, a circumstance likely to have been true for the urban-rural division in the Roman world at large and one which marks in part the generally favoured status of urban slaves. Even at Rome, however, male slaves appear to have preponderated over females : an investigation of the burial sites of three aristocratic households from the early imperial age has revealed a ratio of two male slaves to every

---

(93) FESTUS, *De uerb. signif.*, p. 118 Lindsay ; cf. PLATNER, ASHBY (1929), s.v.

(94) In Egypt it is difficult to identify slave fathers ; see *P. Brux.* E 7360 and *P. Ryl.* 178, two examples where slave men had free wives. Paternity of infant slaves did not of course have to be officially recorded, a fact which indicates an attitude of general relevance : an owner was under no constraint, legal or otherwise, to recognise the existence of a slave family. But it does not follow that 'fatherless' slave children were always the product of casual sexual relationships, as perhaps implied for an earlier period by P. M. FRASER, *Ptolemaic Alexandria*, Oxford, 1972, I p. 85.

(95) See above, n. 87.

female, though the imbalance may not have been representative of
conditions in the city, or other cities, as a whole ; although many infant
females were kept and raised for later work in the domestic entourages of
their owners, others were exposed, either to be left to die or to be claimed
by whoever might want them, because it was uneconomic to have
excessive numbers of young females in the household [96]. Nonetheless
female slaves there certainly were, since the private retinues of Roman
grandees required substantial numbers of both men and women to
perform the needed highly specialised services and to add to the lustre of
the magnate [97]. Slave women were also involved to some extent in the
commercial life of Rome [98]. The result may well have been that there
was a certain competition among male slaves for the number of potential
wives available when marriage was being contemplated, a factor which
may, on the male side, have sharpened the value of a successfully
achieved union. Furthermore, the relative shortage of female slaves may
offer one reason why such women were very young, by modern
standards, when they married, their husbands usually being much older
than themselves [99]. However that may be, men and women were able in
their selection of a partner to benefit both from the huge size of urban
households and from the proximity of such households to one another. It
has been shown that slaves tended to marry from the same household [100]
and the reasons for this pattern are not hard to find : the slaves enjoyed a
greater chance of spending time together than if they were from separate
households, while sanction of marriage from the owner could be expected
since he would benefit materially from any offspring the slaves might
produce (whether it was kept or sold). Yet to a lesser degree marriages
between slaves of separate households are attested [101], and that fact
presupposes a certain willingness on the part of owners to cater to servile
interests.

(96) TREGGIARI (1975b), 395. See also Appendix C for earlier information.

(97) Cf. DION. HAL. 4.24. On services in the grand *familiae* see TREGGIARI (1973) ;
(1975a) ; (1976), 76ff.

(98) Susan TREGGIARI, *Lower Class Women in the Roman Economy* in *Florilegium* 1
(1979), 65ff.

(99) On the age at which females married see HOPKINS (1965) ; WEAVER (1972), 184 ;
186.

(100) WEAVER (1972), 192 ; cf. also FLORY (1978). Some male slaves owned their female
slaves, *uicariae*, regarded presumably as wives on occasion ; see for example *ILS* 7981a ;
7981b.

(101) WEAVER (1972), 191 ; TREGGIARI (1975b), 398.

Accurate proportions cannot be given, but it is probably true to believe that male slaves engaged in farm work of one kind and another far outnumbered those found in the cities ([102]). And little is heard of female slaves in the rural sector : in the works of the agricultural writers, for example, they scarcely appear at all, with the exception of the *uilica*. But this silence should not be taken to signify a total absence of slave women from rural society, a point which requires emphasis ([103]), because in spite of the absence of prolific epigraphical testimony characteristic of Rome and other cities there are indications that opportunities for servile family life in the country were far from hopeless. For a period as early as the late second century B.C. there is evidence that slaves who had been imported to Italy from overseas to meet labour demands in Italian agriculture had reproduced in sufficient numbers so as to become a cause of public alarm ([104]). There is no reason to doubt this information, which strongly implies the availability to slave men of women since the status of a child followed that of the mother ([105]). Indeed, legal sources point towards the presence of women on farms, and it is significant that a catalogue of traditional occupations for slave women given by Plautus includes shepherding ([106]). Nearer the beginning of the imperial age Virgil tells a tale of an Italian *pastor* who, late in life, exchanged a spendthrift female companion, seemingly of long-standing, for one more frugal, a story told without any sign that the relationships mentioned were extraordinary ([107]). In Petronius' *Satyricon*, the realistic substratum of which is certain, Trimalchio receives news of servile births on his estates at Cumae ; the married couple on Juvenal's farm outside Rome has already been mentioned, and a passage in the *Digest* indicates availability of slave

(102) The majority of the population in antiquity was always occupied in agriculture ; cf. Veyne (1961), 228 ; Hopkins (1967), 166f.

(103) It has been claimed that the 'Roman writers of treatises on agriculture imply that in the period of expansion agricultural slaves were usually male and celibate' ; Hopkins (1978), 106 (see also Hopkins (1967), 170 ; 171 : 'on plantations, certainly, male slaves were kept apart, without families'). This view seems to minimise the texts from Varro and Columella referred to at the beginning of the chapter and is to be questioned. Contrast Martin (1974), 290, 'La procréation des esclaves ruraux était loin d'être un phénomène négligeable'.

(104) App. *BC* 1.7, though this does not mean of course that breeding fully met labour requirements ; cf. Harris (1979), 84.

(105) Buckland (1908), 397f.

(106) See Brunt (1971), 144 n. 1 ; 707, citing *Dig.* 33.7.12.5 especially, and Treggiari (1979b), 196ff. on *fundus cum instrumento* ; Plaut. *Merc.* 509.

(107) Virg. *Ecl.* 1.27-32.

women on estates in Africa ([108]). Moreover, there are some inscriptions which record slave marriages and families in rural contexts : a male slave described as an *actor et agricola* who died at the age of forty was commemorated by his surviving slave wife on a stone from Velitrae, while an inscription from Gaul referring to a husband, wife and son who were all slaves commemorates the husband and father, dead at forty-one, a man who had also been a rural *actor* ([109]). Finally, there is some evidence of slave child labour in the country, young people who might reasonably be assumed to have been born there, especially in view of Varro's statement that births increased the farm owner's estate ([110]).

In any case the silence of Varro and Columella on slave women is not total, as already seen, and is explicable : it can be attributed to the fact that the labour skills of women were not suited to the farm work with which the agricultural writers were principally concerned ; the domestic and commercial skills provided by slave women in cities were not required to the same degree in the country. All the same there will have been a need for clothes-making, cooking, cleaning, tending children and so on, occupations strictly outside of the interests of Varro and Columella, but when the context is appropriate remarks are forthcoming ([111]). Moreover, in order to explain the preponderance of male over female slaves in Rome, the attractive suggestion has been made that girls were deliberately taken away from the urban households in which they were born and put on farms precisely for the purposes of domestic work and subsequent childbearing ([112]). Altogether, therefore, there is no cause for believing that slave marriages and families did not exist in rural situations ([113]), only for believing that female availability as wives for men was far more limited

(108) Petr. *Sat.* 53.2 ; Iuv. 11.146ff. ; *Dig.* 33.7.27.1 ; cf. Gsell (1932), 401, and see also Mart. *Epig.* 12.18 (Bilbilis) ; Tibullus 2.1.23, *turbaque uernarum, saturi bona signa coloni.*

(109) *ILS* 7451 ; 7452.

(110) See above n. 37 for Varro, and note particularly *RR.* 2.1.26, cited in n. 16 ; cf. Brunt (1958), 166.

(111) Varro, *RR.* 2.10.7 on the best kind of women to have for the mates of the *pastores.* Col. *RR.* 12.3.6 has been taken to suggest the common presence of women on farms (e.g. Martin (1974), 290) but this text is arguable ; (cf. also Col. *RR.* 8.2.7).

(112) Treggiari (1975b), 400 ; (1979b), 189f. This view becomes even more useful if it is true to believe that deaths resulting from female infant exposure were minimal ; cf. above n. 35. Moreover, country life was good for human reproduction, according to Apul. *Apol.* 88.

(113) Contrast Finley (1976), 820 ; Harris (1980), 119f.

than in cities and that the feasibility of achieving marriage and producing children was consequently more difficult. Not that all male agricultural labourers were themselves suitable for the concession of family life : those dangerous or uncompliant enough to warrant being housed in the *ergastula* can presumably have had little expectation of normal family life. In turn, the exclusion or deprivation of some may once more have increased the value of marriage and children to those fortunate enough to have had them.

The lowest expectations of family life were faced by male slaves who worked in the mining districts of the Empire. The work itself, gruelling and dangerous, allowed for no female presence in the labour force ; the turn-over of male labourers seems to have been rapid due to a high mortality rate [114] ; and the criminal penalty of condemnation to the mines was not applied to women [115]. None of these conditions favoured the formation of family units, let alone maintenance of stability within them. It would perhaps be too sweeping to claim that the slave family did not exist at all among mining slaves. Diodorus Siculus' description of the gold mines in Egypt contains references to women and children, and the charter of Vipasca, a mining community in Spain formally organised in the reign of Hadrian, has a provision for the use by women of the public baths [116]. But Diodorus is describing Egypt before its annexation by Rome and the women referred to in the charter of Vipasca are more likely to have been the free residents of the community than slaves. On balance the family will have been a rare phenomenon among slaves who worked in mines.

A factor which worked in favour of servile familial stability was manumission, the acquisition of freedom by slaves, which brought among other things release from anxieties about separation from family members [117]. From inscriptional evidence it is possible to see various stages of the securing of freedom by family units which had come into being after two people had married while slaves, but which had been affected by the death of one of the principals. A male slave may have been set free by his owner, for instance, and have subsequently gained his

(114) See O. DAVIES, *Roman Mines in Europe*, Oxford, 1935, 14ff.
(115) On *metallum* see in general GARNSEY (1970), 131ff.
(116) DIOD. SIC. 3.12.2-13.2 ; *ILS* 6891.
(117) Since manumission is the subject of Chapter III the remarks here are restricted to the relationship between family life and freedom.

wife's freedom so that he became her patron. The pattern is illustrated by the example of a slave named Heracla who took his former master's praenomen and nomen upon manumission to become L. Volusius Heracla ; his wife Prima later took her husband's nomen, becoming Volusia Prima, and on Heracla's death she made a dedication to her *coniunx* and *patronus* [118]. The children of parents such as these might themselves have also been set free, as seems to have happened with a brother and sister named Cn. Racilius Fructuosus and Racilia Fructuosa, whose mother, Racilia Eutychia, also set up a memorial to her deceased *patronus* and *coniunx*, Cn. Racilius Telesphorus [119]. In instances of this sort both children and parents had escaped the dangers of familial severance and emotional disruption. But not all were so fortunate. Of the family of L. Volusius Hamillus, clearly a freedman, his wife Ianuaria and son Hamillus were still slaves apparently (to judge from the single names) when their husband and father died [120], and their future together will still have been theoretically uncertain. All kinds of permutations were possible. A generous owner might have liberated a married couple simultaneously ; a slave woman might have been set free before her husband, or have become her freed husband's patron, or the patron of her children [121]. It is well understood that masters were agreeable to setting slave women free before the formally required age in order for them to marry [122], yet at the same time it remains true that the majority of slaves in the Roman slavery system never achieved manumission at all [123].

The evidence of the inscriptions thus illustrates the movement of slave families along a sliding scale, as it were, from totally servile status for the whole group to totally free status. The important point, however, is that any progress along the scale depended on the willingness of the owner to liberate one or several family members, a variable which was always beyond absolute prediction. Slave family members were set free and

(118) *ILS* 7413.

(119) *ILS* 8219. It is possible that the children had been born after the manumission of the parents which would automatically have made them freeborn. In this instance the couple had been married for more than twenty-one years, and the son, who died before his father, had not survived to the age of eleven.

(120) *ILS* 7405.

(121) E.g. *ILS* 8162 ; 8259 ; 8388.

(122) Weaver (1972), 186 ; Harris (1980), 120.

(123) Hopkins (1978), 118 ; 139. Examples of no family members achieving freedom at the time principals were commemorated appear in *ILS* 7404 ; 7423 ; 7430.

families could reach a level of stability ; but when two slaves first married they had no way of assuring or controlling their future family life. The advantages which manumission brought the slave family were constantly the prerogative of the master, and that knowledge must again have always formed another aspect of the slave mentality and consciousness which in turn modified the behaviour of the slaves themselves ([124]).

The encouragement of slave family life by owners and their willingness to separate the members of slave families when necessary form two opposing but not mutually inconsistent tendencies. Given the complexity of the Roman slavery system, indeed, it would be surprising if historical analysis of it could be reduced to neat and fully congruent lines. Slaves in the Roman world attached as much importance to family life as other sections of society and they desired if possible to create and maintain their own family units. In many cases this was achieved, both across time and space, but always through the agency of their owners, who understood directly the principle that allowing the formation of slave families contributed to the achievement of contentment and hence acquiescence among their slaves. Stability in slave families, however, was shaped, and to some extent undermined, by factors arising from the mechanics of the slave-owning system, which constantly exposed slaves to the danger of familial disruption because of their disposable nature as a form of property. Owners exhibited no reluctance or qualms about causing separation when occasion demanded because the purpose of the slave family had been served up to the time of disposal and separation, while for the new owners of transferred property other avenues of manipulation were available ([125]).

The value slaves attached to family ties was high, and owners were able to exploit to their advantage the element of uncertainty in slave life which was produced by the inevitable transference of slaves in normal social and economic circumstances. Opportunities for marriage and family life were far from equal among slaves but depended in part on their location within

(124) If the manumission of one partner in a slave marriage entailed departure from the household, then freedom would have had a negative impact on his family life ; this must have happened sometimes (cf. TREGGIARI (1969), 209) but as always its precise extent is difficult to evaluate.

(125) It may be true that 'The legal attitude to slave families became gradually more humane under the empire' ; TREGGIARI (1979b), 196. But this view seems to me to be overly generous ; in any case, the opinions of jurists are not necessarily an accurate index of historical reality.

the range of servile statuses, in part on the type of household to which they belonged, in part on the availability of marriage partners, in part on owners' readiness to manumit. Those factors in themselves perpetuated divisions among the slave population at large and thus served the interest of maintaining the social status quo. All in all the family life of slaves fortunate enough to enjoy it was always precarious until the complete family had acquired emancipation, and indirectly it was in this element of precariousness that owners' psychological control over their property was able to make itself felt most forcefully. The response of slaves to this reality, it might be imagined, was to demonstrate attitudes of acquiescence and passivity in order to protect and preserve as far as possible the familial associations they were able to bring into existence.

CHAPTER III

MANUMISSION

Manumission was always a distinctive feature of the Roman slavery system and has a history that stretches back well before the imperial period ([1]). Roman masters were indeed relatively liberal in the extent to which they conferred freedom on their slaves, and at any moment innumerable ex-slaves throughout the Roman world demonstrated by their mere existence that slavery was not of necessity a permanent state but one from which release was possible. The freedmen and freedwomen of Roman society provided for those still in slavery an example to follow and emulate.

It should be noted immediately, however, that when slaves were set free they did not in consequence find themselves absolved of all responsibilities towards their former owners, now patrons. Instead, as a condition of release from servile status the freedman might find himself bound to his patron by a nexus of obligations, summed up in the legal term *operae*, as a result of which he continued to discharge various services for the patron for a certain length of time ([2]). This device was convenient to both parties, because it meant that the social status of the slave could improve dramatically but without the automatic accompaniment of economic loss to the owner who still benefited from the freedman's efforts on his behalf. To some degree the system of *operae* explains the prevalence of manumission in Roman society as a whole ([3]).

In spite of these restrictions it is absolutely clear that slaves coveted freedom and were anxious to become whenever possible part of the great mass of ex-slaves. The advantages were obvious : in theory at least all subjection to the whim of the slave-owner disappeared, the acquisition of

---

(1) Cf. Dion. Hal. 4.24.1-4 and see in general Watson (1971), 43ff. ; (1975), 86ff.

(2) For *operae* see Duff (1958), 44ff. ; Treggiari (1969), 75ff.

(3) For a recent account of Roman manumission practices see Hopkins (1978), 115ff., which may not, however, be compelling in all respects ; cf. K. R. Bradley, *CP* 76 (1981), 82ff.

Roman citizenship brought political and legal rights, descendants had before them the prospect of upward social mobility. In reality the ex-slave forfeited upon manumission the economic support of his former master and henceforward had to rely on his own efforts in order to provide basic necessities ; it was possible, therefore, that hardship in the former slave's life could replace a certain material security, as shown by the following passage from the philosopher Epictetus, himself an ex-slave :

> Then he (the slave) is emancipated, and forthwith, having no place to which to go and eat, he looks for someone to flatter, for someone at whose house to dine. Next he either earns a living by prostitution, and so endures the most dreadful things, and if he gets a manger at which to eat he has fallen into a slavery much more severe than the first ; or even if he grows rich, being a vulgarian he has fallen in love with a chit of a girl, and is miserable, and laments, and yearns for his slavery again. "Why, what was wrong with me ? Someone else kept me in clothes, and shoes, and supplied me with food, and nursed me when I was sick ; I served him in only a few matters. But now, miserable man that I am, what suffering is mine, who am a slave to several instead of one !" (Epict. *Diss.* 4.1.35-37, Loeb translation).

But as far as can be told slaves seem in general not to have been deterred by this possibility, which must often have been realised, from seizing the new status once it was within their grasp. Indeed inscriptions from slaves who had successfully escaped their original servile condition illustrate the importance they attached to the acquisition of freedom. There is a certain pride visible, for instance, in dedications recording the discharge by free men of vows undertaken as slaves, in dedications 'on behalf of freedom', and in a plain but emotive expression of the type 'C. Ducenius Phoebus, freedman of Gaius, son of Zeno, was born at Nisibis in Syria and became a free man at Rome' [4].

Since no precise statistics on the total population of the Roman world and on the servile proportion of it exist, the extent of manumission in different times or places cannot be measured ; obviously, however, variations should be expected depending, as far as numbers are concerned, on the relative incidence of slave-owning throughout the

---

(4) *ILS* 3427 ; 3491 (cf. 3819) ; 3526, *ob libertatem* ; 3944, *C. Ducenius C. lib. Phoebus, filius Zenonis, natus in Suria Nisibyn, liber factus Romae* ; cf. also *CIL* 6.663, a prayer to Silvanus, *ob libertatem*. For evidence from an early date that slaves aspired towards freedom see PLAUT. *Amph.* 462 ; *Aul.* 817 ; 824 ; *Capt.* 119f. See also PHAEDR. *Fab.* II 5 for servile degradation encouraged by the hope of manumission.

empire (⁵). Yet the motives which led masters to confer freedom on slaves seem to have remained consistent over time and place : owners were concerned to attract the esteem of their peers through acts of apparent kindliness, to act generously for its own sake (not to be minimised), or else to reward slaves in return for meritorious service and the personal demonstration of loyalty and obedience over the years (⁶). Again these are factors which contribute to understanding why so many slaves in the Roman world were set free, but it is with the notion of freedom as an incentive and reward in the life of the slave that attention here is concerned, a notion illustrated in Columella's statement, quoted earlier, that he had rewarded with freedom a slave woman who had borne at least four sons for her owner (⁷). Not only had the woman added to the number of slaves in Columella's overall possession, but during the years in which her children were being produced she must also have demonstrated little opposition to her servile status. After her reward, it is easy to see how her life can have operated as a prototype for her fellow-slaves — acquiescence to the will of the owner would bring similar compensation in time, or so it could be hoped.

Columella was not of course the only slave-owner to appreciate the value of emancipation, or its prospect, as an incentive towards or reward for compliant behaviour in slaves. The principle was understood throughout society and from an early date : the understanding that freedom could be used both to bribe and repay slaves is apparent first in Plautus and then all manner of literary sources (⁸). But the fact remains that in spite of Rome's liberal practices most of the servile population probably never achieved freedom at all (⁹). Thus the conditions under which slaves might anticipate freedom and the circumstances under which freedom actually proved to be forthcoming need to be delineated so that their connection with the maintenance of stability in Roman society

---

(5) See ALFÖLDY (1972), 110ff. Even the exhaustive study of manumission practices at Delphi in the last two centuries B.C. given by HOPKINS (1978), 133ff. does not permit knowledge of absolute numbers. For regional variations in slave-owning see above, pp. 16f.

(6) See in general Treggiari (1969), 11ff. Emphasis must again be laid on the point that acts of generosity by owners were exceptional not the rule ; cf. FINLEY (1980), 122, and HOPKINS (1978), 117 : 'Roman society was not marked by altruism'.

(7) COL. *RR*. 1.8.19 (see above, p. 51), itself no evidence of disinterested generosity.

(8) E.g. PLAUT. *Cas*. 283f. ; 291ff. ; *Merc*. 152 ; *Poen*. 134 ; SEN. *Ben*. 3.23.2-4 ; *Dig*. 40.2.9.

(9) HOPKINS (1978), 118 ; 139.

can be better understood. Freedom was the greatest reward a slave could
be given, and the factors which governed its acquisition are of cardinal
importance for comprehension of the master-slave relationship.

Manumission was controlled by law, and at the very beginning of the
imperial period Augustus was responsible for the passage of new
regulations which are germane to the subject at hand. In turn, Augustus'
legislation formed a response to circumstances under which slaves had
been set free in the late Republic, so something of that background must
be described before the law itself is examined. As noted above, the Roman
tradition of freeing slaves was very old, but in the last century or so of the
Republic that tradition had been ruthlessly exploited by aspirants to
political power : the revolutionary period had created a climate in which
slaves in Rome and Italy could be and were offered their freedom,
randomly and opportunistically, by men immersed in war and politics
who needed all possible support to further their public ambitions. While it
would be superfluous to list all the relevant examples, from the tribunate
of Gaius Gracchus until the battle of Actium, a few may be mentioned to
show the tendency at work by which slaves were offered freedom at
moments of crisis and upheaval in return for their political or physical
support ([10]). Thus, Gaius Gracchus and his associate C. Fulvius Flaccus
are said to have made an offer to slaves at Rome in the tumult which
preceded their own deaths ; in 89 B.C. the senate en bloc offered freedom
as a reward to any slaves who would bring information to light on the
assassination at Rome of the praetor A. Sempronius Asellio ; at the battle
of the Colline Gate slaves were offered freedom for their support of the
Marians against Sulla, who himself was later said to have liberated ten
thousand men to serve as his own personal bodyguard ; and L. Cornelius
Cinna twice offered slaves their freedom at times of civil commotion ([11]).
In a later era Sex. Pompeius used the offer of freedom for slaves' help
against their masters in Africa ; the members of the second triumvirate
offered the rewards of freedom and cash to slave informants ; and

---

(10) For the background see H. KÜHNE, *Zur Teilnahme von Sklaven und Freigelassenen
an den Bürgerkriegen der Freien in I. Jahrhundert v.u. Z. im Rom* in *StudClas* 4 (1962),
189ff. ; cf. WESTERMANN (1955), 66f. The significance of offers of freedom is highlighted
by the contrast with economic pressures which could be applied to tenant-farmers, but
which could not be used with slaves ; cf. M. I. FINLEY, *Private Farm Tenancy in Italy
before Diocletian* in M. I. Finley, ed., *Studies in Roman Property*, Cambridge, 1976, 103ff.
at pp. 115f.

(11) APP. *BC* 1.26 ; 54 ; 58 ; 65 ; 69 ; 74 ; 100.

Octavian was said to have liberated some twenty thousand slaves to serve as rowers in the campaign against Pompeius, claiming himself in the *Res Gestae* to have restored to their owners thirty thousand slaves who had absconded to fight in the late civil wars on the promise of manumission ([12]).

It is possible that in the often confused political and military circumstances of the late Republic slaves took the opportunity to liberate themselves without direct provocation from the ruling elite, for at the time of the Catilinarian conspiracy it is likely that slaves outside Rome who were not actively recruited for rebellion used the occasion of civil unrest to make themselves free ([13]). However that may be, it is very clear that these offers of freedom, of which there were many more than those mentioned, acted as powerful motivating forces, and they offer strong evidence of slave-owners' awareness of the importance of freedom in the servile mentality. The offers were not always taken up by the slaves ([14]) : over successive generations slaves periodically showed themselves not altogether devoid of political acumen by realising that promises of freedom could not always be guaranteed. But the final result was that the frequency with which the offers were made destroyed whatever balance there might otherwise have been between masters and slaves as far as manumission was concerned and confusion was substituted for it : there was no stable basis on which slaves could put their expectations and the impact on slave psychology must have been severe. Despite Cicero's famous remark that slaves might expect to be manumitted after seven years of enslavement, there are no grounds for believing the statement to be generally valid ([15]).

At the close of the Republic then, there was a long history of strained relations between masters and slaves, the outcome of the formers' abuse of manumission for self-interested reasons, of which, it should be observed, Augustus himself had firsthand experience. This situation was aggravated further in the period of Caesar's ascendancy through the early years of Augustus' principate by new accretions to the servile population

(12) App. *BC* 4.7 ; 11 ; 36 ; 95 ; 131 (cf. 73 ; 81) ; Suet. *Aug.* 16.1 ; Caes. *BC* 1.57 ; Dio 41.38.3 ; *RG* 25.1 ; Oros. 5.12.6.

(13) See K. R. Bradley, *Slaves and the Conspiracy of Catiline* in *CP* 73 (1978), 329ff.

(14) E.g., App. *BC* 1.26 ; 54 ; 58 ; 65.

(15) Cic. *Phil.* 8.11 ; the text contrasts strongly with other evidence (see below, pp. 110f.), and Cicero's description of the slaves needs to be noted, *captiui serui frugi et diligentes*, as another illustration of the expectation of servile acquiescence. Cf. Weaver (1972), 97.

which followed from the military campaigns Rome waged abroad on a vigorous scale and which produced great numbers of captives. During the campaigns in Gaul Caesar took phenomenal numbers of prisoners, over four hundred thousand according to one source [16]. In 25 B.C. forty-four thousand members of the Alpine Salassi are said to have been sold into slavery for a minimum period of twenty years ; in 22 B.C. members of the Cantabri and Astures in Spain were enslaved ; in 12 B.C. the future emperor Tiberius reduced a revolt in Pannonia and sold the men of military age into slavery ; in 11 B.C. members of the Thracian Bessi were also enslaved [17]. The subsequent history of all of these people is not certain, and it should not be automatically assumed that all were imported to Rome and Italy [18]. But there is a strong likelihood that many were : Dio is specific that the Pannonians enslaved by Tiberius were to be deported from their country and Suetonius reports that under Augustus enslaved captives were to remain in servitude for at least thirty years and were not allowed to stay in any country near their own [19]. The contemporary witness Strabo himself saw British captives in Rome [20].

These new acquisitions of relatively unsophisticated slaves from predominantly western and Danubian sources can have done little to improve the insecure relations between masters and slaves in the last decades of the first century B.C. With the gradual establishment of the Augustan peace, however, the uncertain political conditions of the late Republic receded, allowing thereby for the prospect of a new stability between slaves and their owners and in particular for the creation of fixed standards for the award of freedom to slaves. It is in this context that Augustus' legislation on slaves should be seen, and some attention can now be given to this aspect of Augustus' achievement, which represented an effort to establish an official, public set of standards for the granting of

(16) VELL. PAT. 2.47.1 ; cf. PLUT. *Caes.* 15.5 ; APP. *Celt.* 1.2 ; cf. VOLKMANN (1961), 51f.

(17) STRABO 4.6.7 ; DIO 53.25.4 ; 54.5.2 ; 31.3 ; 34.7 ; cf. VOLKMANN (1961), 34 ; 50. Enslavement in the East under Augustus was minimal ; see WESTERMANN (1955), 84.

(18) At later times war captives were sometimes sent to work in mines outside Italy ; for example, Jewish prisoners were sent to Egypt after the war against Rome that began in Nero's reign (Jos. *BJ* 6.418) and captives from Trajan's campaigns in Dacia may have been sent to mines in Dalmatia (see BODOR (1963), 45ff.). For captives as a continuing source of slaves under the empire see STAERMAN-TROFIMOVA (1975), 13ff. ; HARRIS (1980), 121f.

(19) DIO 54.31.1 ; SUET. *Aug.* 21.2.

(20) STRABO 4.5.2.

freedom to slaves to be followed by individual owners in their own households. Once the public posture has been outlined, the more realistic circumstances which lay behind manumission can be compared.

In 2 B.C. the *lex Fufia Caninia* introduced a sliding scale to govern the proportion of slaves in a single household that could be set free at the owner's death ; the proportion declined as the size of the household increased and in no circumstances could more than one hundred slaves be manumitted (²¹). The thrust of the *lex Aelia Sentia* of A.D. 4 was to fix a minimum age of thirty for a slave and of twenty for a slave-owner before manumission with the Roman citizenship could be accepted by one or conferred by the other, though there were some exceptions in both cases (²²). A third law, the *lex Junia*, formalised the half-way status between slavery and full emancipation by allowing freedom without citizenship ; it remains unclear, however, whether this enactment belongs to the reign of Augustus or that of Tiberius (²³).

What was the purpose of this legislation ? In his biography of Augustus, Suetonius offers the following general statement :

> Considering it also of great importance to keep the people pure and unsullied by any taint of foreign or servile blood, he was most chary of conferring Roman citizenship and set a limit to manumission (Suet. *Aug.* 40.3, Loeb translation) (²⁴).

(21) For the sources of the *lex Fufia Caninia* see *RE* 12 cols. 2355-2356 (R. Leonhard). A full account of the Augustan slavery legislation from the strictly legal point of view is provided by BUCKLAND (1908), 537ff. ; cf. also ATKINSON (1966) ; STAERMAN-TROFIMOVA (1975), 216ff. ; ROBLEDA (1976), 149ff. For Augustus' use of intermediaries in lawmaking see DIO 55.13.4.

(22) For the sources of the *lex Aelia Sentia* see *RE* 12 cols. 2321-2322 (R. Leonhard).

(23) For the sources of the *lex Junia* see *RE* 12 cols. 910-923 (Steinwenter) ; cf. also SHERWIN-WHITE (1973), 328ff. ; ROBLEDA (1976), 135ff. For arguments in favour of an Augustan date see LAST (1934), 888ff. ; ATKINSON (1966), 361ff. ; and in favour of a Tiberian date SHERWIN-WHITE (1973), 332ff.

(24) *Magni praeterea existimans sincerum atque ab omni colluuione peregrini ac seruilis sanguinis incorruptum seruare populum, et ciuitates Romanas parcissime dedit et manumittendi modum terminauit.* The generalisation has been doubted by BRUNT (1958), 164, who makes the important observation that freedmen were encouraged by Augustus to propagate (cf. JONES (1970), 133f.), a relevant consideration for estimating the views of LAST (1934) on the Augustan slavery legislation (see Appendix D). Suetonius' text, *ab omni colluuione peregrini ac seruilis sanguinis*, is the only evidence which could possibly be taken to suggest a racial motive behind the slavery laws, but it contains no hint of specific races and cannot support the construction of Last and his followers. It is far more natural to take the text in a social and moral sense.

This is subsequently illustrated first with instances of Augustus' reluctance to make viritim grants of citizenship and then with details on the slavery legislation :

> Not content with making it difficult for slaves to acquire freedom, and still more so for them to attain full rights, by making careful provision as to the number, condition, and status of those who were manumitted, he added the proviso that no one who had ever been put in irons or tortured should acquire citizenship by any grade of freedom. (Suet. *Aug*. 40.4, Loeb translation) [25].

These passages show with certainty that Augustus did not object to the principle of manumission itself, and, given the force of existing Roman tradition and practice, any notion of completely stopping manumission would of course have been impossible. Instead, insistence was made on the suitability of those slaves who could be considered for the citizenship which full freedom brought. In one of the two examples Suetonius gives of Augustus' refusal to grant the *ciuitas*, stress is firmly laid on the point that the person concerned, a Greek client of Tiberius, was not qualified : there were no justifiable grounds for it [26]. The same thought is apparent at the end of the second quotation above [27] : the Roman citizenship was not to be defiled by being bestowed on criminous slaves. It was obviously important in Augustus' thinking to preserve the moral respectability of the *ciuitas*, a view confirmed both by Suetonius' later comments on Augustus' treatment of his own slaves and freedmen who did not know their place [28], and by the evidence of Dio on the slavery legislation.

According to Dio Augustus established minimum ages for slave and master at the time of manumission and instituted rules to govern

---

(25) *Seruos non contentus multis difficultatibus a libertate et multo pluribus a libertate iusta remouisse, cum et de numero et de condicione ac differentia eorum, qui manumitterentur, curiose cauisset, hoc quoque adiecit, ne uinctus umquam tortusue quis ullo libertatis genere ciuitatem adipisceretur.*

(26) Suet. *Aug*. 40.3, *Tiberio pro cliente Graeco petenti rescripsit, non aliter se daturum, quam si praesens sibi persuasisset, quam iustas petendi causas haberet.*

(27) A reference to the provision in the *lex Aelia* concerning *dediticii* ; Gaius, *Inst.* 1.13 ; 14 ; 26.

(28) Suet. *Aug*. 67. On the idea of moral personality see also *Dig*. 40.4.46. Cf. Brunt (1958), 164 on Augustus' wish 'to limit the flow of new citizens to the extent that their *cultural* absorption could be achieved' (Brunt's emphasis). It is not clear whether this means before or after conferment of the *ciuitas*, though from Suetonius and what follows proof of moral responsibility was plainly desired beforehand.

treatment of slaves by their former owners and by the general public [29]. Dio principally (though briefly) refers here to the *lex Aelia*, and his reason for the initiatives is worth noticing : too many people were freeing their slaves indiscriminately [30]. His statement should not be taken simply in a numerical sense but also from a qualitative point of view : there was no barrier to servile emancipation once the requisite qualification had been achieved and it was the moral fibre of the slave to which attention had to be given.

This point has to be spelled out because modern scholarship on the Augustan legislation has been dominated by the idea that in the pre-Augustan era too many slaves, simply, were being manumitted and that Augustus merely wished to halt the numerical flow of emancipations [31]. A passage from Dionysius of Halicarnassus has been customarily invoked in support of the traditional interpretation [32], but in actuality its main concern is the same as that already seen in Suetonius and Dio. Pausing in his account of the reign of the king Servius Tullius, Dionysius digresses on the early practice of manumission at Rome and finds nothing to criticize in that very early period of Roman history. He then contrasts what he considers to be the more lax and unjustifiable procedures of his own day : slaves, he says, now buy their freedom from the proceeds of criminal acts ; they are set free for having served as their masters' accomplices and confidants in crime, or to allow owners to benefit from public largesse or to display their owners' liberality at death [33]. Again Dionysius shows no sign of opposition to manumission itself, only disapproval of manumission for the wrong reasons ; and he makes the constructive suggestion of screening ex-slaves, in the manner of the censorial review of senators and equestrians, to ensure that they maintain a proper moral status [34].

Dionysius is not likely to be inventing false facts in his lament on the manumission procedures of the late first century B.C. ; something of the background due to political factors has already been seen. But qualification must certainly be applied to the literal statement of the extent of 'corruption' in Roman society. First, Dionysius speaks of only a

(29) Dio 55.13.7.

(30) πολλῶν τε πολλοὺς ἀκρίτως ἐλευθερούντων ; cf. ATKINSON (1966), 367.

(31) See Appendix D.

(32) DION. HAL. 4.24.1-8.

(33) DION. HAL. 4.24.4 ; STAERMAN-TROFIMOVA (1975), 216f. emphasise savings the state could make from the distribution of largesse if manumissions were reduced.

(34) DION. HAL. 4.24.8.

minority of slaves for most people, he says, disapprove testamentary manumission for reasons of social ostentation : it is *some* slaves who purchase freedom with illicitly gained cash, *others* who assist their masters in crime ; *some* who are freed for the sake of largesse, *others* for their owners' display. But nowhere does Dionysius complain of *all* slaves being criminals or being set free for defective reasons ; rather he speaks of deviation from morally accepted standards by an unspecified, and unspecifiable, number of people. Secondly, the whole digression is a rhetorical topos on the decline of moral standards of Rome, a comparison of a corrupt present with a better past, the nature of which is purely conventional in Roman literature [35]. In consequence Dionysius should not be taken too seriously. The point is that his text contains no objection to the numerical extent of manumission once the correct kind of behaviour has been exhibited by those slaves to be set free.

It cannot of course be denied that the *lex Fufia* shows some concern with slave numbers, but in spite of Suetonius' comments on restricting manumissions it is not really known if the limits were severe or liberal in comparison with practices in individual households before the law was passed [36], and it is difficult to see how its provisions can have had a great impact on the absolute numbers of slaves being set free after its passage because other methods than testamentary manumission continued to be available. The way was still open for an owner, technically at least, to set free all of his slaves before his death if he wished, a fact which makes it hard to believe that the *lex Fufia* was conceived with a numerical problem alone behind it. Moreover, the *lex Fufia* cannot be interpreted as an attempt to deal with manumission by will and the *lex Aelia* with manumission during the owner's lifetime with an emphasis once more on sheer numbers of slaves [37], because the lapse of six years between the two measures is too great to make any sense of what was a foreseeable situation after the passage of the first law. Had Augustus been driven by no more than a wish to make drastic reductions in the numbers of slaves being freed in 2 B.C., it is far more plausible to imagine that all forms of emancipation would have been dealt with at one fell swoop. Nor, finally,

---

(35) See WILLIAMS (1968), 630f. on moral decline, and cf., for example, COL. *RR*. 12 *praef.* 8-9 ; AMM. MARC. 14.6.16-17. On the numbers question cf. HOPKINS (1978), 128.

(36) Apart from the evidence given in n. 30, Dio says nothing concerning reduction of the numbers of manumissions.

(37) As in DUFF (1958), 31f. ; LAST (1934), 433 ; *RE* 12 col. 2321 (Leonhard).

are there any justifiable grounds for believing that testamentary manumission was more common than other methods [38]; otherwise passage of the *lex Aelia*, which applied to manumission during the owner's lifetime as well as by his will [39], would have been superfluous.

The *lex Fufia* governed testamentary manumission and it is the precise occasion of this form of conferring freedom on slaves which is of most relevance to understanding its intent. The contemporary evidence of Dionysius just summarised, for all its rhetoric, reveals a tendency on the part of the Roman elite to free slaves by will as a form of social ostentation, which in actuality cost the owner nothing, the rationale being to have all think well of the deceased from a final act of generosity. It is known that Augustus endeavoured to regulate other kinds of ostentatious behaviour among the Roman upper classes by sumptuary laws, which placed limits on private spending, extravagance and bribery, and to set a new moral tone in society not least by his legislation on marriage [40]. The *lex Fufia* is best understood in consequence as one of a series of efforts to amend the luxurious and unpalatable practices of the ruling classes by imposing reasonable, but not necessarily stringent, limits on the numbers of slaves who could be freed by will. This is not to deny that some effect may have been subsequently felt on the absolute numbers of slaves who were set free, but if so this was of no more than secondary importance.

A common interest, however, between the two slavery laws can still be perceived. For those slave-owners who were to adhere to the dictates of the *lex Fufia* without setting free their slaves en masse while still alive, a principle of selectivity, imposed from without, must henceforward have made itself felt as they listed in their wills the names of those slaves who would become free once the wills were implemented. When looked at from the servile point of view, one of the effects of the *lex Fufia* was to give testamentary emancipation something of the character of a competition, the rules for which had to be compliant behaviour, loyalty and obedience. The beginnings of a set of standards by which

---

(38) This is a common view among scholars ; see, for example, BUCKLAND (1908), 442 ; 460 ; DUFF (1958), 25 ; ROBLEDA (1976), 121 ; but it is hardly plausible ; cf. ATKINSON (1966), 368 ; TREGGIARI (1969), 27.

(39) GAIUS, *Inst.* 11.17 ; 18.

(40) GELL. *NA* 2.24.14 (cf. 15) ; SUET. *Aug.* 34.1 (cf. 89.2) ; cf. DIO 54.16.3-5. On the marriage legislation see references at p. 48 n. 9. Note that according to *Dig.* 40.2.16 the *lex Aelia* was designed to prevent manumission for reasons of *luxuria*. For the elite luxury of the age see Jasper GRIFFIN, *Augustan Poetry and the Life of Luxury* in *JRS* 66 (1976), 87ff.

manumission could be achieved thus become visible and with the *lex Aelia* the standards at large become much clearer.

The conferment of freedom together with the *ciuitas* is the most significant feature of the *lex Aelia* because in theory the new law did not prevent liberation of slaves below the age of thirty but simply denied them access to fully freed status [41]. The law, it can be emphasised, showed a concern with protecting the moral character of the citizenship but not with delimiting the actual extent of manumission in the sense of merely setting slaves free. It may be in fact that the establishment of an arbitrary age for full manumission, with the citizenship, encouraged servile agitation for it once the requisite age had been reached, since the law was creating reasonable expectation of full emancipation at a definite point in the slave's life. What is of more consequence, however, is that the *lex Aelia* made full manumission a reward to the slave who reached a deserving age, or, once the exceptions to the main rules are examined, a slave who displayed conformity to the established values of free society. Full freedom below thirty was possible in cases involving a blood relationship between master and slave, cases where the slave was the teacher of the owner's children, a potential wife or *procurator* for the owner, or an *alumnus* [42]. In this regard the law exhibited no repressiveness at all but rather encouraged conventional domestic relationships within the household. Moreover, the absolute denial of the citizenship upon emancipation in all circumstances to those slaves to be categorised as *dediticii* by the *lex Aelia* had the corollary effect of instituting a penalty in the absence of meritorious servile conduct [43]. Slaves who, at the time of emancipation, had ever been put in chains, branded, found guilty of a crime after torture, consigned to fight in the arena, or put in the gladiatorial schools, could never achieve full citizen status because the law judged them guilty of moral disgrace (*turpitudo*), though freedom itself was not denied them [44]. It can be plainly stated that the *lex Aelia* conceived of both reward and penalty in moralistic terms (the force of *turpitudo* should be noted especially) and set up a code of

---

(41) GAIUS, *Inst.* 1.17 ; 18.
(42) GAIUS, *Inst.* 1.19 ; 39.
(43) GAIUS, *Inst.* 1.15.
(44) GAIUS, *Inst.* 1.15, *Huius ergo turpitudinis seruos quocumque modo et cuiuscumque aetatis manumissos, etsi pleno iure dominorum fuerint, numquam aut ciues Romanos aut Latinos fieri dicemus, sed omni modo dediticiorum numero constitui intellegemus.*

desired behaviour for the slave, behaviour at once dictated to and fostered in the slave by the slave-owning classes.

It is implicit in the law that slaves wished to acquire the *ciuitas* as much as simple release from slavery, and this is only to be expected as a true reflection of real historical circumstance. Without full freedom the ex-slave might find his condition tenuous, the status and prospects of his children dubious, participation in the life of the community to which he belonged difficult. Under the terms of the law, however, if slaves were to achieve full emancipation they had to ensure for a substantial amount of time, especially those who were homeborn slaves, that all criminal involvement were avoided. Thus the potential reward of Roman citizenship conferred by free society became, from the slaves' point of view, an inducement to sound moral behaviour during the period of enslavement or, in other words, to assimilating themselves within the existing social status quo. This preempted, at least in theory, their participation in acts of rebellion, escape by flight, or any other means of securing freedom not condoned by free society. It may be suggested consequently that the purpose of the *lex Aelia* was to inform slaves as much as their owners of the qualifications required for citizenship, and to create potential for harmony between privileged and non-privileged sections of Roman society by offering slaves the prospect of eventual release from their condition in a way which meantime guaranteed without resistance the continuation of the servile system on which the elite so heavily depended [45].

The provisions of the *lex Junia* may be taken to confirm this view. The creation of Junian status as a half-way step towards full citizenship carried the liability that Junians were debarred from directly benefiting from wills, from making wills of their own, or from being appointed tutors in wills [46]. The converse of these restrictions was the reward that Junians

---

(45) The ideas of reward and penalty in the *lex Aelia* have of course always been recognised ; see for example H. F. JOLOWICZ and Barry NICHOLAS, *Historical Introduction to the Study of Roman Law*[3], Cambridge, 1972, 345 ; SHERWIN-WHITE (1973), 327ff. ; (and cf. LAST (1934), 429, 'moral fitness'). But the question of why such ideas were carried into law has not been given a great deal of attention, though it becomes all the more urgent once alleged motives of numerical restriction of manumissions in and of itself and of avoiding racial fusion are downplayed, as clearly they must be ; see Appendix D.

(46) GAIUS, *Inst.* 1.23. As with the *lex Aelia*, however, an easing of these restrictions meant that Junians could receive legacies through the complicated rules of *fideicommissum* ; GAIUS, *Inst.* 1.24.

could acquire full status through what has been called the 'benefit of paternity', meaning marriage and the procreation of children [47]. Here the notions of reward and penalty are again quite explicit : the capacity to receive and to dispose of property is considered by the law as something befitting a citizen only, and the further notion is implicit that additional passage of time after acquisition of Junian status is necessary before the former slave is ready to assume all the citizen's responsibilities. Similarly, the law is liberal to the Junian once commitment to established social values, marriage and the raising of a family, is demonstrated, but once more only after the passage of a certain interval of time, the reaching of age one by a child [48]. From the Junian's point of view, therefore, full citizen rank was made an incentive to greater acceptance of social conformity as imposed downwards from the upper reaches of society, whereas its rejection resulted in the retention of inferior social grade. Junian status was in itself a sign that progress in the social order was possible, but the law continued to protect the citizenship until its recipients were morally suitable for it.

If passage of the *lex Junia* preceded that of the *lex Aelia*, it might perhaps be possible to speak of a broad system devised by the Augustan government to mould the behaviour of slaves and ex-slaves in society as a whole. But if the *lex Junia* is of Tiberian date, it should then be viewed as an extension of a principle first laid down in the *lex Aelia* [49]. Nevertheless, it is true that over the course of the first century and beyond the principle of the *lex Aelia* was gradually extended, as far as Junians were concerned, into a much wider network of incentives which led to full citizen status in return for service to the community which represented thereby further attachment to free Roman values. Service in the *Vigiles* for six years, the furnishing of grain ships, the building of houses at Rome, working in a mill for three years at Rome, all these circumstances were covered in successive enactments up until the reign of Trajan as means of arriving at fully freed status [50]. The consequence of the scheme introduced by the *lex Aelia* and the *lex Junia* was that their

(47) The phrase is from SHERWIN-WHITE (1973), 332 and elsewhere. This is to equate the *Latini* of GAIUS, *Inst.* 1.29 with Junians, which seems necessary.

(48) GAIUS, *Inst.* 1.29 ; ULP. 3.3. It should be noted that the *fideicommissum* provision shows that there was no objection by the makers of the law to ex-slaves receiving legacies ; it merely had to be done by a clumsy and penalising method.

(49) See n. 23 above for sources on the date of the *lex Junia*.

(50) GAIUS, *Inst.* 1.32b-34 ; ULP. 3.1-6 ; cf. SUET. *Claud.* 18.2 ; TAC. *Ann.* 15.43.3.

promulgators, who naturally represented the slave-owning section of society, were deliberately attempting through the use of the law to perpetuate the established social status quo by appealing for the support of slaves and former slaves, whose eventual reward, after the passage of time and proof of acceptability, was assimilation within it.

Something of the background against which the Augustan legislation was passed has already been seen. It can be emphasised finally, however, that it was precisely those new slaves who continued to arrive in Rome and Italy from tribal settings who were most in need of the acculturative programme of incentives, rewards and penalties laid down by the law. By A.D. 4 war captives who had earlier been enslaved for periods of twenty or thirty years would be nearing the time when manumission may have been becoming a real possibility for those who had survived. Yet it is perfectly credible that the Roman authorities still felt the need to guard against admission to the *ciuitas* of elements which had not yet achieved a demonstrable degree of commitment towards Rome and its values. The *lex Aelia*, and possibly the *lex Junia* too, was passed with the social legacy of earlier military conquests in mind as a form of social control in its own right and in a very direct sense.

The Augustan legislation, then, set public standards or conditions for the emancipation of slaves and, although later modified, it remained in effect for centuries, until the time of Justinian in fact [51]. But the difficulty which underlay the slavery laws, as indeed all Augustus' social enactments, was one of enforcement : the creation of public conditions for manumission could not provide any guarantee that in everyday reality they would be met by slaves or maintained by slave-owners. At this point, therefore, an attempt must be made to see how the process of manumission actually operated in the lives of slaves and their masters. It will become clear in the end that the main condition prescribed for slaves by the *lex Aelia*, attainment of age thirty, was only one of a series of barriers to freedom which had to be successfully crossed before emancipation could become a reality.

The first point to make is that it cannot be imagined that waiting for the arrival of age thirty was a simple waiting process for the slave. The unfulfilled anticipation of freedom is recorded in melancholy fashion on an inscription from Venafrum which refers to a slave *uilicus* who died too

(51) *Instit.* 1.5.3 ; 7.

young to be manumitted : *debita libertas iuueni mihi lege negata morte immatura reddita perpetua est* [52]. Although there is no accurate means of calculating life-expectancy for antiquity, it is indisputable that thirty was a far more advanced age than in the modern world, particularly so at the lower levels of society which, in the cities especially, were most affected by overcrowding, disease, poor health facilities and other social misfortunes, and life-expectancy at birth for slaves is not likely to have been much more than twenty years [53]. The survival of a slave to age thirty cannot have been regarded as automatic or easily predictable, and this consideration only reinforces the notion apparent in the *lex Aelia* that manumission was a long-term reward for many years of devoted service from the slave.

Secondly the slave's acquisition of freedom never became a right, no matter what reasonable expectations the law fostered, but depended ultimately on the willingness of the owner to agree to manumission ; as such freedom was subject to the owner's caprice and an owner on his death-bed might be as inclined towards severity as generosity, towards the lash as towards largesse [54]. From a survey of epigraphic evidence from the western provinces of the Empire, it has been contended that slaves between the ages of thirty and forty had a very good chance of being set free [55], but even if this were true there was still no certainty of the fact ; and the mass of tombstones from which servile expectations have been inferred tells only of those slaves who in later life secured sufficient wealth to be able to make some commemoration of themselves and their family members. It cannot be assumed that such expectations presented themselves to all points of the servile compass at all moments in time, and it is more plausible to believe that the majority of slaves was never set free at all [56]. No doubt location to some degree determined slaves' prospects

---

(52) *CIL* 10.4917.

(53) Sepulchral inscriptions which record ages of death have been shown to be of no value for calculating life-expectancy in spite of their abundance ; see M. K. Hopkins, *On the Probable Age Structure of the Roman Empire* in *Population Studies* 20 (1966), 245ff., who nonetheless argues for the whole population an expectation of life at birth of below thirty but over twenty years ; this estimate is conventionally accepted ; cf. Brunt (1971), 132f. ; Engels (1980), 116ff. ; Harris (1980), 118 ; (see also Hopkins (1978), 34 n. 44). On urban problems see P. A. Brunt, *The Roman Mob* in *Past & Present* no. 35 (1966), 3ff. = M. I. Finley, ed., *Studies in Ancient Society*, London, 1974, 74ff.

(54) Cf. Tac. *Ann.* 16.19.4, *seruorum alios largitione, quosdam uerberibus adfecit.*

(55) Alföldy (1972), 114f.

(56) See above n. 9.

of emancipation [57], but in all cases agreement of the master had to be gained beforehand and this was a factor always subject to denial or withdrawal. As a passage in Tacitus makes clear, the conferment of freedom on a slave was a *beneficium* which followed evidence of servile *obsequium*, an act of generosity which resided in the control of the master alone, not of the slave [58].

Although the evidence is limited in quantity, enough documentary records of manumission are available to illustrate the element of personal inclination at work on the master's part, to the disadvantage of the slave. The will of Dasumius, first of all, provides a glimpse into the liberation of household slaves by a member of the Roman upper crust early in the second century. The text is too fragmentary to allow the total number of manumitted slaves to emerge but that is relatively unimportant. What is remarkable in the will is the express ban on the setting free of a certain group of slaves at any future point in their lives after Dasumius' death, a prerogative which was, indeed, formally sanctioned by the law [59] : 'I ask', Dasumius writes, 'that Menecrates and Paedaros not be manumitted but kept in the same occupation as long as they live ... because they have given me great offence by their lack of merit' [60]. It was observed earlier that the *lex Fufia* is likely to have imposed a principle of selectivity upon owners intending to manumit slaves by will, but in this particular instance the master went beyond that constraint to leave certain members of his household little hope whatever of ever leaving their servile condition.

As a complete contrast to the harsh attitude of Dasumius, the generosity of an anonymous slave-owner from Egypt appears in a fragment of his will, appropriately governed, it is clear, by the *lex Fufia*, in which he asks that some of his slaves be set free despite the fact that they had absconded [61]. It may perhaps be doubted that slave-owners were regularly prepared to overlook such recalcitrant behaviour in their households since efforts were often made to recapture and punish fugitives [62], and it was

(57) See further below, pp. 103ff.

(58) Tac. *Ann.* 13.26.4-5.

(59) *Dig.* 40.1.4.9 ; 40.1.9.

(60) *FIRA*² III no. 148, lines 80ff., *Menecraten et Paedaro[tem rogo ne manumittas, sed in eodem o]pere illos habeas donec ui[uent, quo habui ego ... quoniam n]ullo merito meo tam ualde [offenderunt...].*

(61) *P. Hamb.* 1.72 = *CPL* no. 174 ; for the legality of the procedure, *Paul. Sent.* 4.14.3. For manumission documents from Egypt see Biezunská-Małowist (1977), 145.

(62) See, for instance, *P. Oxy.* 1422 ; 1423 ; 1643 ; cf. above, p. 32.

probably more normal that slaves were liberated 'on account of their goodwill and affection' towards the owner, a phrase which appears in Egyptian documents that highlight the demonstration of appropriate servile conduct before conferment of the reward [63]. But when freedom was bestowed the master was still able if he wished to impose restrictions on it. For example, in the will dating from the mid second century of Acusilaus [64], a resident of Oxyrhynchus, five female slaves were set free but subject to the condition that their services and earnings were to remain after Acusilaus' death at the disposal of his wife as long as she survived, while his son was given claim to any children borne by the women in the future. Not all of Acusilaus' slaves were liberated in the will : some went again to the son, though the wife had a right to sell or mortgage them if she wished. Inevitably, the reading of a will must have brought a certain disappointment to those not fortunate enough to be on the manumission list.

In the well-known will of a veteran of the Roman fleet which belongs to the late second century [65], C. Longinus Castor gave freedom to two female slaves, Marcella and Cleopatra, both of whom are described as being over thirty and who in actuality were to become Castor's heirs, as well as to Cleopatra's daughter Sarapias. Four other individuals are named in the document, probably slaves, but nothing is said of their emancipation. In a case such as this it is likely that the slaves knew in advance of their impending manumission, once the owner died that is : in Petronius' novel, indeed, Trimalchio announces his intention to his favourite slaves of setting them free in his will and of giving them property [66]. Wills were by no means the last minute dictates of slave-owners but were often drawn up years before death finally occurred. Longinus Castor's will was made in 189 and opened in 194, Acusilaus' was made in 156 and opened in 165, while the younger Pliny refers to a

---

(63) κατ' εὔνοιαν καὶ φιλοστοργίαν ; *P. Oxy.* 494 ; *P. Tebt.* 407 ; cf. BIEZUNSKA-MAŁOWIST (1977), 116f.

(64) *P. Oxy.* 494 = A. S. HUNT, C. C. EDGAR, *Select Papyri* I (LCL 1932), no. 84. For forms of manumission in Egypt under local as well as Roman law see TAUBENSCHLAG (1955), 96ff. ; MONTEVECCHI (1973), 201f. ; cf. also M. W. HASLAM, *Notes on Deeds of Manumission* in *ZPE* 20 (1976), 58ff.

(65) *BGU* 326 = A. S. HUNT, C. C. EDGAR, *Select Papyri* I (LCL 1932), no. 85 = *FIRA*² III no. 50.

(66) PETR. *Sat.* 71.1-3.

will made eighteen years before implementation [67]. To earn the initial favour of the master, however, and thus to become a candidate for testamentary manumission, total subordination of the slave to the interests of the master was required, subordination which could then be maintained by the owner through making known in advance the contents of his will. This procedure resulted in a guarantee of continued compliance on the part of the slave, extending over an indefinite interval of time and which for the slave meant more years of waiting before freedom became a reality. Slaves who hoped for liberation in this way had to ensure that they became the 'dearest' slaves within the household [68], whether or not genuine sentiment was involved, and that they remained so by continued self-denial and conformity. Even so, changes made in wills when periodically revised could still confound expectations, and there was also always the chance that wills could be disregarded : in the late second century in Egypt a letter was sent by a certain Marsisuchus to his wife and daughter threatening them not to interfere with arrangements he had made for setting free a number of slaves [69].

In the last resort of course slaves were able to commit acts of violence against their owners if they believed their own interests had been injured, though this does not seem to have happened frequently to judge from the surviving literary record [70]. What might take place, however, is illustrated by Tacitus' famous account of the murder of the city prefect L. Pedanius Secundus at the hands of a slave in 61 [71]. Tacitus did not know the precise cause of the attack on Pedanius Secundus but he gives as a possible motive the explanation that an agreement on a price for manumission had been made between the prefect and the slave, but that Pedanius had reneged on the contract at the last minute [72]. It is of some significance that this could occur to Tacitus as a rational account of the episode since presumably it would also have been comprehensible and

(67) PLIN. *Epp.* 8.18.5 ; cf. 5.5.2 ; the contents of an old will did not always reflect the testator's final wishes.

(68) TAC. *Ann.* 15.54.2, *carissimi*.

(69) *P. Tebt.* 407 ; the wife and daughter may have already had some claim on some of the slaves (BIEZUNSKÁ-MAŁOWIST (1977), 95). Cf. SHERWIN-WHITE (1966), 320, on revising wills.

(70) See below, p. 113.

(71) TAC. *Ann.* 14.42-45.

(72) TAC. *Ann.* 14.42.1, *seu negata libertate cui pretium pepigerat*. Cf. *Dig.* 40.1.5, the slave was supposed to seek redress before the city prefect or provincial governor when his owner reneged on a manumission agreement.

acceptable to his readers ; as such the explanation might suggest that Pedanius' behaviour was not all that unusual. What was abnormal was the slave's recourse to violence, when resignation to the master's decision would perhaps be more normally forthcoming.

If the passage of time and the caprice of the master were circumstances beyond the direct control of slaves, there were also other practical hurdles to be confronted and crossed before the process of manumission could be brought to completion. For formal emancipation during the lifetime of the owner to be valid, both master and slave had to appear before a Roman magistrate for the ceremony of liberation to take place ([73]). The magistrate concerned could be a consul or, more usually, a praetor at Rome, and in the provinces a proconsul or imperial legate, or even an imperial procurator ([74]). In Egypt the local agoranomus of a town was often involved with manumissions subject to Greco-Egyptian rather than Roman law ([75]). Certain legal texts suggest that these occasions could be very casual affairs and this has been taken as a sign of the frequency with which manumissions occurred ([76]). Thus Gaius states : 'Slaves over thirty can usually be set free at any time, so that they are manumitted for instance when the praetor or proconsul is en route to the baths or the theatre' (*Inst.* 1.20). But the context of this passage shows that Gaius is drawing a contrast with the fixed days on which slaves below the age of thirty were able to appear before the appropriate board to prove their grounds for exemption from the normal rules in order to be set free, and it is equally clear that Gaius' text was copied wholesale or adapted by subsequent jurists, which means that mere repetition of the statement does not give it any greater force as a piece of historical evidence ([77]). At most, therefore, the legal texts should be taken to signify the constant potential availability of manumission, but they are not in themselves evidence of constant frequency of manumission.

---

(73) See Buckland (1908), 451ff. on manumission *uindicta*.

(74) Buckland (1908), 453 (under some circumstances local officials were acceptable).

(75) Taubenschlag (1955), 97f. ; cf. A. H. M. Jones, *The Cities of the Eastern Roman Provinces*², 1971, 317ff.

(76) Gaius, *Inst.* 1.20 ; *Dig.* 40.2.7 ; *Instit.* 1.5.2 ; Alföldy (1972), 105f.

(77) Gaius, *Inst.* 1.20, *in prouinciis ... idque (consilium) fit ultimo die conuentus ; sed Romae certis diebus apud consilium manumittuntur. maiores uero triginta annorum serui semper manumitti solent, adeo ut uel in transitu manumittantur, ueluti cum praetor aut pro consule in balneum uel in theatrum eat.*

The agreement of the master always had to be secured for emancipation and then the relevant magistrate approached. This may have been relatively straightforward in Rome itself when local slaves and their owners did not have to travel a great distance to find the urban praetor, who, however, even in the imperial period had other responsibilities than presiding over manumissions [78]. But outside the city the situation was rather different. The younger Pliny provides a case in point in a letter addressed to his wife's grandfather L. Calpurnius Fabatus [79], who apparently wished to complete the manumission of a number of Junians on his estate in northern Italy but was hampered by the lack of a suitable magistrate. Pliny wrote that his friend Calestrius Tiro was about to assume a governorship of one of the Spanish provinces and could be persuaded to visit Calpurnius Fabatus for the purpose on his way out. In the sequel Calestrius complied and the operation was brought to a successful conclusion [80]. But the fortuitous set of circumstances required for this to happen – Pliny's initial willingness to intervene on the Junians' behalf (there was certainly no compulsion to do so) and the subsequent willingness of a magistrate to make himself available when he happened to be in the vicinity of Calpurnius Fabatus' estate – is revealing : it was not necessarily easy for the administrative apparatus of manumission to be set in motion. Pliny also later assisted three other Junians whose patron he had become through the will of another friend by requesting full emancipation for them from Trajan ; again the outcome was successful, though Pliny deliberately overlooked the claims to full freedom of other Junians from the same estate [81]. A forty year old Jewish woman who was set free with her two young children at Oxyrhynchus in the late third century through the process of *manumissio inter amicos* was again fortunate to be ransomed from slavery through the efforts on her behalf of the membership of a local synagogue [82].

In the provinces, indeed, the administrative complications were great. Formal manumissions were part of the regular round of business of the provincial governor : in the political crisis of 68 the future emperor Galba distracted himself from affairs of state by presiding over manumission

---

(78) See Th. MOMMSEN, *Römisches Staatsrecht* II³, Leipzig, 1887-88, I, 193ff.
(79) PLIN. *Epp.* 7.16 ; cf. SHERWIN-WHITE (1966), 420f.
(80) PLIN. *Epp.* 7.32.1.
(81) PLIN. *Epp.* 10.104-105 ; cf. SHERWIN-WHITE (1966), 714f. Cf. MART. *Epig.* 9.87.
(82) *P. Oxy.* 1205 (291).

cases, having issued an edict to appoint a day on which individual manumissions would be granted [83]. But access to the governor by the slave was not possible at any given moment. In the imperial period it was the governor's practice during his term of office to make circuit tours of his province, residing temporarily in those cities which had the status of an assize centre, so that administrative and judicial business was handled locally but only for a relatively short interval in each place [84]. Several months might pass before a slave who had been promised freedom could expect the governor to be on hand for the formal ceremony to occur, and even then it was not automatic that his case would be taken up because the governor had a great deal of latitude in deciding to which matters he would give attention [85]. In addition not every city in a province was an assize centre ; so candidates for emancipation might be compelled to travel with their owners to an appropriate city when they were not themselves resident in an assize centre, and it may be wondered how often owners were willing to sacrifice time, money and effort on travel and indefinite attendance on the governor for the purpose of formally setting free their slaves. Popular complaints about the inconveniences caused by the circuit tour system were not unknown [86]. The whole operation was thus unpredictable and in bringing it to a successful end from the servile point of view, any number of adverse factors might intervene to scotch the whole process. Application of these factors is likely to have intensified when a slave who claimed to be free and who found his claim disputed took the option theoretically open to all imperial subjects and presented a petition to the emperor himself for resolution of his situation. A compilation of evidence from the major law codes has revealed that in the Antonine and Severan periods especially successive emperors certainly dealt with such petitions, and for the most part decisions were handed

(83) Suet. *Galba* 10.1 (cf. 9.2) ; Plut. *Galba* 5.1.

(84) Sherwin-White (1966), 640 ; Burton (1975), who examines the practices of proconsuls only, though it should not be doubted that imperial legates also conducted assize tours, as Pliny in Bithynia (even though Pliny's was an unusual imperial appointment). Note the inclusion in *Dig.* 40.2.7. of *legatusue Caesaris* and in *Instit.* 1.5.2 of *praeses*, in contrast to Gaius' omission (*Inst.* 1.20) ; and for the prefect of Egypt's tour see G. Foti Talamanca, *Ricerche sul processo nell'Egitto greco-romano* I, Milan, 1974, with *Dig.* 40.2.21 for the prefect's ability to preside over manumissions (from the time of Augustus).

(85) Burton (1975),100f.

(86) Dio Chrys. *Orat.* 35.17.

down in favour of the slave petitioners [87]. But the volume of such appeals is never likely to have been large, because access to the emperor by any subject was drastically limited by considerations of space, time and money, the social status of the petitioner, and the emperor's selection of business items [88].

In the way, seen earlier, that the family lives of slaves were to some degree governed by their geographical and occupational location, so too were slaves' prospects of acquiring freedom. It should be expected that urban domestic servants, who had close contacts with their owners, would be able to win the attention and favour of owners and thus present good claims for emancipation, especially if their jobs were rather more than simply menial. In his biographies of Roman grammarians Suetonius presents one type of slave who could benefit from the value attached to literary accomplishments and he preserves the information, for example, that Staberius Eros, a Thracian slave, was set free 'on account of his zeal for literature', and Lenaeus, a freedman of Cn. Pompeius, 'on account of his wit and learning' [89]. The use of ex-slaves in positions of responsibility and slaves' acquisition of freedom from the basis of such occupations as nurse, pedagogue and doctor are features of the Roman slavery system too familiar to warrant elaboration [90]. Manumission of agricultural slaves, who did not have the same kind of proximity to their owners, often absentees, is less well attested and as far as can be told even the *uilicus* on the farm was probably a slave more often than a freedman [91]. One reason

(87) PIGANIOL (1958); cf. MILLAR (1977), 10f. Piganiol showed the tendency for freedom to be ratified when circumstances were dubious and explained it in terms of humanitarian, philosophical influences on the Antonine and Severan emperors. This may be doubted and it is alternatively possible that verdicts favourable to slaves were given for reasons of creating good public relations. If imperial decisions were continually given against petitioners the result would have been general servile antagonism ; instead it was more important that freedom be seen to be attainable. Nothing was lost by the conferments while the benefit to society at large was considerable. Cf. the practice of habitual manumission in the circus at Constantinople, AMM. MARC. 22.7.2.

(88) MILLAR (1977), 465ff. ; cf. WYNNE WILLIAMS, *The 'Libellus' Procedure and the Severan Papyri* in *JRS* 64 (1974), 86ff.

(89) SUET. *Gramm.* 13, *propter litterarum studium manumissus* ; 15, *ob ingenium atque doctrinam gratis manumissus.*

(90) DUFF (1958), 89ff. ; VOGT (1975), 103ff.

(91) WHITE (1970), 352 is perhaps overly cautious about manumission among rural slaves (contrast p. 358) ; see also TREGGIARI (1969), 106ff., who did not have to mention Columella's reference to emancipation of the prolific slave-woman. On *uilici* see MARÓTI (1976), 115ff., and Rhona BEARE, *Were Bailiffs Ever Free Born ?* in *CQ* 72 (1978), 398ff., who gives *CIL* 3.7147 (Tralles) and *ILS* 7372 (Atina) as examples of bailiffs being set free.

why little is heard of rural emancipation will be that those who gained it will have been probably less able, for financial reasons, to commemorate themselves with inscriptions than freedmen in cities, though the odd example survives, such as that of a freed *pecuarius* mentioned on a stone from Moguntiacum, and although Virgil's Tityrus is a fiction, its basis cannot be totally unrealistic [92]. Even slaves who worked in the harsh conditions of the mines, and who can rarely have escaped, had the possibility of emancipation before them, to judge from the charter of Salpensa in Spain (belonging to the eighties of the first century) in which detailed provisions for local manumission are set down in such a context that mining slaves must be understood to be catered for [93]. While, therefore, gradations of expectation of freedom are indisputable, it was important that hope of freedom be made available to all slaves, no matter what their status, so that during slavery their behaviour could be regulated and exploited.

Location was also important for the slave's personal accumulation of cash with which freedom might be purchased from the owner, but before that theme is pursued the importance in the Roman slavery system of manumission in the provinces can be underscored from examining some details about the tax collected by the Roman state when formal emancipation took place, the *uicesima libertatis*. This tax has a very long history indeed, extending from the mid fourth century B.C. as far as the fourth century A.D., which in itself is a reflection of the value of the tax as a continuing source of public revenue over the centuries. Many aspects of the administration of the tax are no more than imperfectly understood, but it is clear enough that in the imperial age it was collected on an empire-wide basis. The find-spots of inscriptions which commemorate persons involved with the *uicesima libertatis* should not perhaps be automatically regarded as evidence of tax collection in those areas, but it is likely that most inscriptions were set up in places where tax-agents had worked, and once these areas are set alongside those for which the evidence of collection is unquestionable, it can scarcely be doubted that all formal manumissions were subject to the *uicesima* in all regions where Roman law prevailed. The evidence covers Spain, Gaul, Bithynia-Pontus-

---

(92) *ILS* 8511 ; Virg. *Ecl.* 1.27-35 ; cf. Eleanor Windsor Leach, *Virgil's Eclogues*, Bloomington, 1974, 119ff. ; Williams (1968), 307ff. ; note also *Dig.* 40.4.52, *testamenta paganorum*.
(93) *ILS* 6088.28.

Paphlagonia, Egypt, Dacia, Achaea, Germany, Africa, Asia, and of course Rome and Italy ([94]).

There is something of a tendency in recent scholarship on slavery to stress that from an economic standpoint at least only classical Italy, not the Roman empire *in toto*, can be accurately categorised as a genuine slave society ([95]). While such emphasis has value in certain respects, it has the corollary effect of minimising the significance of slaves elsewhere which in other respects was considerable. The fact that slaves in Roman Egypt constituted less than twenty percent of the full population ([96]), for example, may mean that Egypt was not a true slave society, but it can hardly follow that formally manumitted slaves in Egypt, or anywhere else, were of no consequence as far as Roman financial administrators were concerned. Roman government did not differentiate between genuine and non-genuine slave societies within the overall empire, but from the fiscal point of view regarded all slaves everywhere in an identical manner.

It is also noteworthy that the manumission tax was still being collected in the fourth century when slavery as a system of compulsory labour was being overtaken by the colonate ([97]). It is not difficult to see why when there still remained great numbers of slaves in the Roman world and when manumission was still being practised. The apparent liberation of some eight thousand slaves by the Christian Melania early in the fifth century may not have been a typical event ([98]), but the proceeds of even lesser acts of generosity will still have been worth collecting. The action of the emperor Caracalla in temporarily doubling the *uicesima libertatis* and the sense of urgency apparent in a letter concerning the tax written by a prefect of Egypt in the second century ([99]) suggest that Rome was always interested in collecting revenue from manumissions and that money was always there to be collected. The long chronological duration of the tax

(94) See Appendix E for evidence on the chronology and collection of the *uicesima libertatis*.

(95) HOPKINS (1978), 99 ; FINLEY (1980), 9 ; 79.

(96) HOPKINS (1978), 99 ; (1980), 329f.

(97) For the background see A. H. M. JONES, *The Roman Colonate* in *Past & Present* no. 13 (1958), 1ff. = *The Roman Economy* (ed. P. A. Brunt, Oxford, 1974), 293ff. ; FINLEY (1980), 123ff.

(98) FINLEY (1980), 123, rightly emphasising previous underestimation of the slave population in the later imperial period.

(99) DIO 77.9.4 ; *P. Oxy.* 2265.

and its geographical dispersal can be seen as means by which the Roman state exploited slavery to its own advantage, in this instance purely pecuniary.

Sustained collection of the *uicesima* implies that formal emancipations continued to take place, in the provinces and at Rome, despite the difficulties involved. That is not in contention of course, though the difficulties are not thereby made less in trying to form an estimate of slaves' thinking about and securing of manumission. Indeed, in cases where slaves themselves were responsible for paying the manumission tax ([100]), a financial obstacle to freedom was imposed upon them, which in many instances was added to the problem of accumulating money required for the purchase of manumission itself. It was remarked earlier that testamentary emancipation did not entail financial loss to the slave-owner (though his heirs of course may have been affected). But the situation was rather different when masters freed slaves during their own lifetimes, because they lost both property and the revenue from it. In part the loss was offset by the obligations towards the patron by which the slave was bound on emancipation ([101]), and in wealthy households, where a constant supply of servile births helped keep up the numerical level of the establishment, it is doubtful that Roman magnates suffered unduly in economic terms. Yet even men of senatorial rank needed to be careful about their finances. The younger Pliny was most concerned that a group of slaves he was considering for purchase be inexpensive to maintain ([102]), so in cases of smallscale slave ownership the freeing of slaves can be supposed to have incorporated a certain loss of capital. It consequently causes no surprise that slaves sometimes received their freedom at a price, a mechanism which was obviously designed to compensate the owner. In theory the system was not unreasonable from both points of view : on one hand the slave had before him the incentive of freedom towards which he could aspire through diligence, industry and frugality ; on the other the owner benefited from the collaborative efforts of the slave while a slave and then received a cash dividend when the slave was set free. In practice, however, the system is likely to have been weighted in the interests of the owner, as can be seen to some extent from considering actual costs of emancipation.

(100) See Appendix E for the evidence.
(101) See above n. 2.
(102) PLIN. *Epp.* 1.21.2 (*frugi*, cf. CIC. *Phil.* 8.11).

Very few manumission figures have been preserved by the sources and their typicality is thus open to question. But they allow some slight indication of the financial burden to slaves which the acquisition of freedom might involve. Petronius gives HS4,000 as one figure ; HS10,000 was paid by a dancer named Paris who belonged to an aunt of the emperor Nero ; and HS50,000 was paid by a slave doctor who subsequently took the name P. Decimius Eros Merula [103]. These are considerable sums and fall within the range of attested purchase prices for slaves ; indeed, the cost of manumission probably came close to or was a little higher than the market price of slaves, known for Rome and Italy to have extended from a minimum of HS600 to a maximum of HS700,000 [104]. Purchase prices must have varied according to the skills and ages of the slaves concerned and the same variation is likely to have applied to manumission costs. But it is difficult to see how the vast majority of slaves ever had opportunities to acquire substantial sums of money because most never found themselves in contexts where cash on the grandscale was readily forthcoming. On a recent estimate HS1,000 could provide basic rations for one man for a period of four to eight years, and in the second century the Roman legionary soldier received annual pay of only HS1,200 [105]. This kind of information gives a useful comparison for the manumission figures and strongly suggests that sums of cash had to be accumulated over very lengthy periods before enough was on hand to buy freedom. The chances for saving must have depended on the nature of the slave's occupation or of the household to which he belonged or both. The examples of Paris and Merula indicate that attachment to a large household or expertise in a specialised occupation could produce wealth of considerable dimensions, and slaves who worked as doorkeepers, actors, doctors, prostitutes and so on had jobs which gave a potential for collection of tips and other windfall gifts [106]. Moreover,

---

(103) See DUNCAN-JONES (1974), 349f. ; add PLIN. *NH* 7.128-129 (credible ?). It may perhaps be doubted that sums paid by the slave for manumission were as vital to the Roman slavery system as suggested by HOPKINS (1978), 131 ; 147 ; 160 ; 170 ; cf. K. R. BRADLEY, *CP* 76 (1980), 82ff.

(104) DUNCAN-JONES (1974), 349f. ; HOPKINS (1978), 134 ; WESTERMANN (1955), 36 ; for prices in Egypt see STRAUS (1973) ; BIEZUNSKÁ-MAŁOWIST (1977), 165ff. The range of prices now available in Diocletian's Price Edict is between 10,000 denarii and 30,000 denarii ; *ZPE* 34 (1979), 177.

(105) DUNCAN-JONES (1974), 10 ; 12.

(106) Cf. COL. *RR*. 1.9-10 ; HOR. *Sat.* 1.2.55-56 ; 9.57 ; TAC. *Ann.* 16.11.3. Contrast MART. *Epig.* 2.68, a claim that freedom was purchased at the cost of *totis sarcinis*.

some slaves received wages for their work, a fact illustrated by a papyrus
from the late second century which records the arrangements made
between a female slave-owner in Oxyrhynchus and a local weaver who
was to teach the woman's slave his craft [107]. Whereas the owner
assumed responsibility for feeding and clothing her slave during the four
years of the apprenticeship, the slave was to be paid a regular wage by the
weaver, the amount increasing each year. Technically the wages must
have belonged to the owner who could have reimbursed herself for her
slave's expenses; but it may also be that the slave was allowed to keep
some of the money, perhaps to be saved for eventual manumission. But
most slaves fell outside these circumstances, especially those in agriculture
and mining, and their prospects of acquiring money were consequently
restricted. The importance of the element of time involved here seems to
be shown by two documentary examples of manumission again from
Egypt: in one, from the late first century, a homeborn female slave
named Euphrosyne was set free by her owner (Aline) on payment of a
ransom sum (plus tax) at the age of thirty-five, while in the second,
another woman named Zosime was manumitted by her owner
(Tasucharion) in the late second century, after payment of ransom, at the
age of forty-four [108]. Neither act of emancipation is likely to have been
motivated by pure kindness on the part of the owners.

Monies acquired by the slave became part of his *peculium*, and in
estimating the likelihood of slaves' capacity to buy freedom it is relevant to
consider briefly this feature of the Roman slavery system. In the imperial
age the term *peculium* had come to refer specifically to cash or property at
the disposal of the slave [109]. Technically the *peculium* belonged to the
slave-owner, but in practice the slave usually had complete use and
control of its contents [110], which varied enormously: cash, food,
livestock, land, clothing, moveables, other slaves, even grazing rights are
all attested [111]. And there was no limit on the type of slave who might
have a *peculium*; in exceptional circumstances even slaves in relatively
humble occupations were able to build up impressive holdings: on his

(107) *P. Oxy.* 1647. For similar documents cf. Biezunská-Małowist (1977), 85ff.
(108) *P. Oxy.* 2843 (see also *P. Oxy.* 48); *SB* 6293.
(109) Buckland (1908), 187ff.; Crook (1967), 188f.; see also Finley (1973), 64f.
(110) Buckland (1908), 187; Crook (1967), 189.
(111) Varro, *RR*. 1.17.5; 2.10.5; *Dig.* 15.1.7.4; cf. *RE* 19 cols. 13-16 (W. von
Uxkaill).

arrival at Constantinople in 361 the emperor Julian was amazed at the extravagant attire of a palace barber who, on request, accounted for his 'income' as follows – the equivalent each day of twenty times the daily supply of food for himself and for pack animals, besides an annual salary and other perquisites ; according to the barber, the palace cooks and other servants did just as well [112].

From the evidence of the agricultural writers it could be said that the *peculium* was in its own right a further instrument by which servile interests were met and which contributed towards the creation of good relations between slave and free [113]. The uninterrupted control of cash and property represented a concessive attitude from the master who as always was not obliged to permit existence of the *peculium*, which itself gave the slave some sense of responsibility and some taste of independence. Yet this was not mere and indiscriminate generosity for its own sake on the part of slave-owners : much of the commercial life in Roman society was conducted by slaves exploiting their *peculia* on behalf of their owners, while the diversity of wealth ownership among slaves, comparable and related to the diversity of their statuses and occupations, aided the prevention of any sense of corporate identity among them [114].

Moreover, the slave's *peculium* cannot have been in many cases a bonus, as it were, but a vital part of his basic needs. Although it was the master's responsibility to feed and clothe his slaves, this was not always an easy task for those of relatively modest means [115]. Varro refers to animals kept by slaves on the farm as a means of their being more easily able to maintain themselves, and presumably the animals could provide a source of clothing as well as of food [116]. Thus, an ex-slave who wrote on an epitaph that he was wealthy in spirit even though his *peculium* was small must have been typical of many others at large [117]. Further, it cannot be

---

(112) AMM. MARC. 22.4.9-10 (cf. G. W. BOWERSOCK, *Julian the Apostate*, Cambridge, Mass., 1978, 72) ; VARRO, *RR*. 1.17.5 ; 2.10.5 ; ATH. 6.274d ; VIRG. *Ecl*. 1.27-35. Cf. TREGGIARI (1979b), 200 on *peculium ancillae*. WHITE (1970), 359 doubts the possibility of rural slaves having the *peculium* in Cato's time, but note PLAUT. *Asin*. 539-41, *Etiam opilio qui pascit, mater, alienas ouis, aliquam habet peculiarem, qui spem soletur suam*. When a slave was set free by will, it was possible that his *peculium* was given him by his owner ; for the technical details see BOYER (1965), 360ff.

(113) VARRO, *RR*. 1.17.5.

(114) FINLEY (1973), 64.

(115) SEN. *Ben*. 3.21.2 ; IUV. 3.166-167.

(116) VARRO, *RR*. 1.19.3 ; cf. DIO CHRYS. *Orat*. 7.32.

(117) *ILS* 8436.

imagined that freedom was the only item on which slaves would spend whatever money they had. From epigraphic evidence it appears that at times they spent what must have been substantial sums on commemorative epitaphs and even public monuments ; and money could always be squandered on such luxuries as prostitutes [118]. Nevertheless, when essential and other needs had been met, whatever additional cash could be saved by the slave could go towards the cost of his freedom. Literary sources suggest that slaves went to some lengths to secure cash, as in the case of Tityrus, Virgil's shepherd figure who sold sacrificial animals and cheeses he had made in a local town ; selling off surplus food from the master's table seems to have been possible for domestics, to judge from a story in Apuleius ; and Seneca refers to slaves deliberately starving themselves in order to increase their personal incomes [119]. The proceeds of the *peculium* thus gave the long-term prospect of freedom established by law a short-term immediacy and reality, because cash savings in hand at any one time were a tangible reminder of that distant prospect. The *peculium* acted to reinforce the incentive aspect of manumission.

All in all, however, the simple fact of the slave's ability to purchase his freedom conceals the difficulties actually involved in raising the cash, with the result, again, that freedom was more easily realised by some slaves than others, even though the law, in setting up the abstract conditions under which freedom was to be granted, did not differentiate between one category of slaves and another. Naturally slaves might find themselves rewarded with manumission in return for exceptional acts of loyalty, or the reverse, sooner than anticipated, and the tendency to emancipate women for the purpose of marriage has already been noted [120]. Yet it may be suspected that the kind of career illustrated by the fictional Trimalchio was far closer to the level of reality on which many slaves lived. Trimalchio had come to Italy as a boy from an indeterminate part of Asia and had remained in slavery for fourteen years before, so it seems, he was manumitted in his owner's will, manumission having

(118) Iuv. 3.131-134. For the costs of monuments see DUNCAN-JONES (1974), 79ff. ; 127ff. ; note *ILS* 8265, *Hoc monumentum ex mea frugalitate feci.*

(119) VIRG. *Ecl.* 1.27-35 ; APUL. *Met.* 10.13-14 ; SEN. *Epp.* 80.5 ; cf. also TER. *Phorm.* 43-44.

(120) See above, p. 92. By the early imperial period certain stories about manumission for exceptional acts of loyalty had become canonical (above, pp. 36f.) ; that did not exclude the possibility of other similar eventualities. For offers of freedom for untoward purposes, note APUL. *Apol.* 46, freedom in return for perjury. Cf. *Dig.* 40.2.9.

depended on his ability to secure the favour of both master and mistress during the period of enslavement ([121]). Subsequently the way was open for seeking a fortune, though in reality this did not always lead to the sort of financial success Trimalchio encountered. One ex-slave who is commemorated on an inscription from Naples was set free at the age of thirty-one – on his deathbed ; another who received freedom at the age of thirty in his owner's will survived for little more than a year to enjoy his new condition ([122]).

As far as freedom and manumission are concerned, it can be said that the life of the slave in the Roman world was controlled on two planes : one, the official climate of opinion created by the legislation of Augustus which was developed and maintained by his successors ; the second, the more immediate world of the slave as shaped by his own environment. The law set up rules by which the slave could live his life under the expectation that freedom would be forthcoming once the requirements of age and moral suitability, synonymous with the espousal of Roman values, had been met. Freedom was a long-term prospect, but one that was not wholly beyond reach. In actuality, however, and distinct from the qualifications stipulated by law, the achievement of manumission depended on factors well beyond the slave's control. The elements of time involved – having to survive until the requisite age, having to await the death of the master for testamentary emancipation, having to wait for the accumulation of cash within the *peculium* to buy freedom ; the location of the individual slave in the spectrum of servile statuses ; and above all, the caprice of the slave-owner ; all of these factors conditioned the eventual acquisition of liberty and made it a far more difficult proposition than the strict letter of the law suggests. The fact of the extensive practice of manumission does not alter the situation that manumission was a real but fragile prospect for slaves, and it conceals the years of hardship that preceded its attainment.

From the point of view of the slave-owning establishment, the dual system of control operated in such a way as to maintain acquiescence

(121) Petr. *Sat.* 75-76 (cf. in general Veyne (1961)) ; cf. the biography of the eunuch Eutherius in Amm. Marc. 16.7.5.

(122) *ILS* 7842 ; 1985. It should be remembered that a slave whose freedom was purchased may not have paid the money himself ; it may instead have been paid for him by a family member already free ; this was probably a common phenomenon, but it did not minimise the waiting factor.

among slaves, who did not wish to prejudice their chances of acquiring freedom, and to perpetuate the slavery system to its own advantage. Everything combined to produce subordination in the slave to the master during slavery and to create a situation in which total domination over and exploitation of the slave were feasible. The long-term incentive of freedom did not automatically convert itself for the slave into the final reward, and was not necessarily supposed to, so that as with the family lives of slaves, it was the element of uncertainty which surrounded manumission which made freedom an effective form of social manipulation ([123]).

(123) An incentive does not always have to be applied in order to be effective from the instigator's point of view ; cf. E. J. Hobsbawm, *The Age of Capital 1848-1875*, New York (Mentor edition), 1979, 239, 'The promise of the field-marshal's baton in every private's knapsack was never intended as a programme for promoting all soldiers to field-marshals'.

CHAPTER IV

FEAR, ABUSE, VIOLENCE

In preceding chapters some examples have been examined of ways in which Roman slave-owners might treat their slaves with various forms of generosity, and certain restricting factors which affected their application have been noted. Generosity in and of itself, however, was not enough to secure the elite ideal of servile *fides* and *obsequium*, that is to guarantee social stability, a fact perhaps most blatantly demonstrated to owners on those occasions when slaves became so discontented that they resorted to the ultimate means of defiance and physically attacked their owners. 'No master can feel safe because he is kind and considerate', the younger Pliny aptly commented, on the death in 108 of the praetorian senator Larcius Macedo, who had been assaulted by his slaves while bathing in his villa at Formiae (¹).

No slave-owner wished to be murdered by his slaves, in his bath or elsewhere. Instead it was desirable that slaves stand in fear of their masters (²). Generosity had to be tempered with either force or the threat of force in order for control to be maintained, and a climate of fear over those of subordinate social position had to be created. The principle was well understood in Roman society : Cicero stated bluntly that 'severity must be employed by those who keep subjects under control by force – by masters, for example, towards their slaves, if no other way is possible' (³). Fear in the slave produced greater loyalty, so it was said (⁴), and Columella thus pragmatically advised the prospective buyer of an estate to make a

(1) PLIN. *Epp.* 3.14. For similar episodes compare the murders of L. Pedanius Secundus in 61 (TAC. *Ann.* 14.42-45) and of Afranius Dexter in 105 (PLIN. *Epp.* 8.14). On Pliny's accounts see SHERWIN-WHITE (1966), 246ff. ; 461ff.

(2) Cf. CIC. *Para. Stoic.* 5.41, *omnis animi debilitati et humilis et fracti timiditas seruitus est* ; FINLEY (1976), 820.

(3) CIC. *Off.* 2.24, *Sed iis, qui ui oppressos imperio coercent, sit sane adhibenda saeuitia, ut eris in famulos, si aliter teneri non possunt.* SEN. *Epp.* 4.4 suggests that masters' behaviour could drive slaves to suicide.

(4) PROPERT. 3.6.6, *maioremque timens seruus habere fidem.*

purchase which would allow him to arrive unexpectedly, because his slaves would stay at work because of the fear (*metus*) which resulted [5]. Similarly Tacitus attributes to the jurist C. Cassius in the senatorial debate which followed the servile murder of L. Pedanius Secundus the argument that fear (*metus*) was especially needed among slaves in Nero's reign in view of the admixture of foreigners [6]. All of this was merely a variation on the broad theme, 'Experience teaches that fear is the most effective regulator and guide for the performance of duty', words found in the preamble to Diocletian's Edict on Maximum Prices [7]. Moreover, the all-pervasive quality of this attitude is reflected in early Christian writings, for the reiteration in Apostolic and post-Apostolic literature that slaves should obey their masters 'with fear and trembling' [8] simply shows how Christian leaders absorbed and indirectly supported the ideology of the slave-owning classes in Roman society at large. In this chapter, therefore, some of the ways in which fear might make itself felt in the life of the slave will be presented through describing various forms of abuse and violence to which the slave was exposed as part of everyday normality, the psychological impact of which can subsequently be compared with the results of apparently generous and humane treatment already seen.

Certain kinds of maltreatment which were not punishments but which essentially depended on the exploitation of the slave as a marketable commodity were associated with the slave-dealer (*mango*), and they can be introduced first. In view of his disreputable stock character the slave-dealer is not a figure well represented in surviving literary or other sources, but individuals such as the Toranius Flaccus and A. Kapreilius Timotheus already encountered must have been far more numerous and far more vital a part of the economic life of the Roman world than the sparse record suggests [9]. One reason for their relative obscurity is that, like Trimalchio, men who trafficked in slaves did not necessarily confine

(5) Col. *RR*. 1.2.1.

(6) Tac. *Ann*. 14.44.

(7) *et semper praeceptor metus iustissimus officiorum inuenitur esse moderator* ; line 130 of the preamble in the edition of Marta Giacchero (Genoa, 1974), I p. 136, though the words are outside the narrow context of the master-slave relationship. The origin of the fable is ascribed by Phaedrus (*Fab*. III prol. 33-37) to slaves' fears of speaking openly before masters in case of punishment ; see Appendix F.

(8) *Eph*. 6.5 ; *I Pet*. 18 ; *Did*. 4.11 ; *Barn*. 19.7. For slaves and fearfulness in Plautus, see *Amph*. 291ff. ; *Pseud*. 1103ff. ; *Most*. 859ff. and below, p. 136.

(9) Cf. above, pp. 61f. Evidence is collected in *RE* 14 col. 1107 (Hug), and an inventory of actual dealers is given by Harris (1980), 129ff.

themselves to dealing in one commodity alone but combined slave-dealing with other ventures [10]. In consequence, and given the constancy over time of a regular trade in slaves [11], it can safely be inferred that the abuses for which dealers became notorious, and which restricted their individual self-advertisement, were practised on a wide scale and affected the lives of considerable numbers of slaves.

Slave-dealing was a profitable enterprise [12], and anything which might increase his profit was attempted by the dealer. Slaves put up for sale on the auction block were not always physically excellent specimens, and because the potential purchaser was able to inspect the merchandise before buying [13], dealers tried to disguise defects in order to complete a transaction. For example, a false but healthy looking complexion could be produced in a slave by painting his face, and a thin slave could be artificially fattened up by rubbing an ointment made from terebinth resin over his body so that his skin became loose and enabled a greater intake of food (or so it was believed) [14]. Among other indignities slaves on the block might find themselves being examined for epilepsy, having to appear naked, having their feet whitened with chalk to show their foreign origin, or being obliged to carry placards advertising their own qualities [15]. Moreover, the dealers also catered to the market for slaves as homosexual partners, boys who had to be especially presentable when up for sale. Thus special depilatories were used for the removal of body hair, the growth of which (again so it was believed) could even be prevented [16]. Similarly, ants' eggs, blood from the testicles of castrated lambs and the bodily application of hyacinth bulb dipped in sweet wine were considered to restrain the onset of puberty [17]. Most tellingly of all,

---

(10) PETR. *Sat.* 76.6 ; HARRIS (1980), 129.

(11) M. I. FINLEY, *The Black Sea and Danubian Regions and the Slave Trade in Antiquity* in *Klio* 40 (1962), 51ff.

(12) Cf. CIC. *Orat.* 232. No distinction is made here between primary and secondary dealers, for which see J. P. V. D. BALSDON, *Romans and Aliens*, London, 1979, 78f.

(13) SEN. *Epp.* 80.9.

(14) QUINT. *Inst.* 2.15.25 ; PLIN. *NH* 24.35.

(15) PLIN. *NH* 35.199 ; 201 ; cf. PROPERT. 4.5.52 ; IUV. 1.111 ; cf. *Dig.* 21.1.31.21. SEN. *Epp.* 80.9 ; APUL. *Apol.* 44 ; SUET. *Rhet.* 1.

(16) PLIN. *NH* 32.135. On the connection between homosexuality and slavery see Beert C. VERSTRAETE, *Slavery and the Social Dynamics of Male Homosexual Relations in Ancient Rome* in *Journal of Homosexuality* 5 (1980), 227ff.

(17) PLIN. *NH* 30.41 ; 21.170.

dealers were associated with the practice of castration despite successive laws forbidding it ([18]).

It is impossible of course to measure the actual extent of any of these practices and trade secrets, especially those at first sight seemingly outrageous but not for that reason to be dismissed. Yet taken together they illustrate the level of sheer personal humiliation, if not physical despoliation, to which slaves could be subjected when they passed through the market. The evidence on slave-dealers is strong enough to show activity throughout the Empire, and slave-markets are also attested on a wide basis ([19]). Thus it can scarcely be doubted that personal degradation from the process of sale was a common servile experience, while for those who had been conveyed to Rome or Alexandria ([20]) or some other major city from remote areas of the Mediterranean world, sale and all that it involved was only the culmination of a train of experiences likely to have had both physically and emotionally debilitating effects : capture, forced migration, deracination. As seen already ([21]), the possibility of being sold was a contingency with which any slave might have to contend, and that possibility is as important as the reality itself for understanding the psychological conditions under which slaves lived.

Secondly, since slaves by definition were at the complete disposal of their owners it follows that they might become the object of capricious sexual abuse ([22]), as the practice of castrating young boys confirms. It has already been suggested that the sexual behaviour of slave wet-nurses was adversely affected by the economic interests of their owners ([23]), and similarly the sale of slaves as prostitutes, both male and female, suggests further another form of degradation founded on economic motives, incorporating not only the trauma of sale but also continuous sexual exploitation for as long as the slave-owner wished ([24]). The process is

(18) E.g. MART. *Epig.* 9.6 ; IUV. 6.373A&B ; for the legislation see below, pp. 128f.

(19) HARRIS (1980), 126ff. For sales at Rome itself cf. SEN. *Const.* 13.4, ... *aliquis ex his, qui ad Castoris negotiantur nequam mancipia ementes uendentesque, quorum tabernae pessimorum seruorum turba refertae sunt.*

(20) For Alexandria and the slave trade, see BIEZUNSKA-MAŁOWIST (1976).

(21) See above, pp. 52ff. Something of the fear in servile life which the prospect of sale aroused may be guessed at from the question 'Am I to be sold ?' put to an oracle as recorded in *P. Oxy.* 1477 = A. S. HUNT, C. C. EDGAR, *Select Papyri* I (LCL 1932), no. 195.

(22) Cf. FINLEY (1976) ; (1980), 95f.

(23) See above, pp. 70ff.

(24) Some information on prostitution is assembled in Fernando HENRIQUES, *Prostitution and Society ; A Survey, Vol. I,* London, 1962, 89ff. ; cf. also Hans HERTER, *Die*

illustrated in principle, despite its comic setting, in the auction and sale to a brothel-keeper of the character Tarsia in the *Historia Apollonii Tyriensis*, and Tarsia's subsequent exposure to a string of clients willing to pay for her services ; Tarsia's ability to protect herself by eloquence, however, is not likely to have been the fate of many prostitutes in real life [25]. The number of slaves who functioned as prostitutes appears to have been great, though the information available is mainly anecdotal ; nonetheless rules on the registration and taxing of prostitutes, and the notoriety of an area such as the Subura in Rome itself must be taken to indicate widespread profiteering at the expense of slaves in no position to choose the nature of their work [26].

It is even more probable, however, that slave-owners gratified their own appetites from among the slaves of their households with no thought of financial gain in mind, and from this perspective the poems of Martial prove to be of interest because they are full of allusions to casual sexual relations between owners and slaves, both heterosexual and homosexual. Thus, the outcome of intrigues between one of Martial's addressees, Quirinalis, and this man's maidservants (*ancillae*) was 'homeborn gentlemen' (*equites uernae*), and another addressee, Cinna, is ridiculed by the poet because his seven 'children' had all in fact been fathered by different male slaves in his household [27]. In other poems, a woman uses her dowry to redeem her lover from slavery, relationships between a master and his *uilica* and maidservants, and between a mistress and her litter-bearers are mentioned, young boys and girls are purchased expressly to serve as sexual partners [28].

Soziologie der antiken Prostitution im Lichte des heidnischen und christlichen Schrifttums in *JAC* 3 (1960), 106ff. and (briefly) Sarah B. Pomeroy, *Goddesses, Whores, Wives, and Slaves*, New York, 1975, 192 ; 201. Note Plaut. *Pseud.* 188ff., for the possible contemporary political allusiveness of which see A. Archellasci, *Politique et religion dans le «Pseudolus»* in *REL* 56 (1978), 115ff. at pp. 119ff.

(25) *Hist. Ap. Tyr.* 33-36 (cf. B. E. Perry, *The Ancient Romances*, Berkeley and Los Angeles, 1967, 314f. ; Duncan-Jones (1974), 253f.) ; cf. also Sen. *Controu.* 1.2.3 ; Mart. *Epig.* 6.66 ; Apul. *Met.* 7.9 ; Dio Chrys. *Or.* 7.148.

(26) E.g., Tac. *Ann.* 2.85.1-4 ; Suet. *Cal.* 40 ; T. Frank, ed., *An Economic Survey of Ancient Rome, Vol. IV*, Baltimore, 1938, 253 (F. M. Heichelheim). Hor. *Epod.* 5.58 ; Propert. 4.7.15 ; Mart. *Epig.* 2.17.1 ; 6.66.2 ; 11.61.3 ; 11.78.11. Note also Plaut. *Poen.* 339f. ; Hor. *Epist.* 1.14.21 ; Mart. *Epig.* 3.93.14f. ; Amm. Marc. 28.4.9. For Egypt see Biezunska-Małowist (1977), 91ff.

(27) Mart. *Epig.* 1.84 ; 6.39.

(28) Mart. *Epig.* 2.33 ; 3.33 ; 4.66 ; 6.71 ; 11.70 ; 12.58 ; 12.96.

The practices referred to evoke no comment of disbelief from Martial (²⁹), but if in actuality the historicity of his anecdotes and allusions may be dubious, that is not an important matter. Rather it is the underlying assumptions which are revealing, because Martial takes for granted the fact that slaves of both sexes and of all ages were objects of casual sexual pleasure, and that the contexts of his poems will reflect reality sufficiently to be understood by his readers. Likewise the Stoic Musonius Rufus makes similar assumptions in criticising the master's lack of self-control in his relationships with slave girls (³⁰). It is possible, therefore, that many slaves in close proximity to their owners had to accept with a certain fatalism that they might be required to cater to their owners' sexual demands. Some may even have welcomed the situation, seeing in it a chance to win their owners' approval and their own freedom as a result. This was the claim of Trimalchio concerning his former master and mistress, and it helps explain why the concubines kept in aristocratic households, such as those of Larcius Macedo, were willing to tolerate their position (³¹). It is equally possible that some slaves became involved in relationships with their owners which were founded on genuine sentiment : marriage between an ex-slave and her patron is accepted as normal in the social legislation of Augustus (though the patron himself might well be an ex-slave) (³²). Yet it remains true that slaves were automatically deprived of individuality and self-respect when they could anticipate becoming their owners' involuntary lovers. Sexual abuse was to be expected by them just as much as other forms of maltreatment, and even in a society where sexual relationships were regarded with a great deal of openness and lack of guilt, there is likely to have been in consequence much dehumanisation at work in slave life about which nothing is heard in conventional sources.

The most direct way in which violence appeared in the life of the slave was through physical chastisement, the normal prerogative of the slave-owner to which there was practically no limit, and few owners would have disputed the axiom that 'one must punish one's slaves according to

(29) BARBU (1963), 67ff. believes that Martial has a certain sympathy for abused slaves, is genuinely indignant about their condition, and that the poems (as Juvenal's) are essentially realistic in their description of servile conditions.

(30) MUSONIUS, p. 66 Hense. See in general TREGGIARI (1979b), 192ff.

(31) PETR. Sat. 75.11 ; PLIN. Epp. 3.14.3 ; cf. also SUET. Vesp. 3 ; HA Marc. 29.10 ; see in general RAWSON (1974).

(32) See above, p. 92.

their deserts' ([33]). Physical punishment was taken for granted and largely unquestioned, a fact revealed implicitly in Tacitus' description of slave-owning customs in Germany, where punishment was surprisingly rare, explicitly by Seneca's broad statement that slaves were treated 'not as if they were men, but beasts of burden' ([34]). In Seneca's view, indeed, owners were in general 'excessively haughty, cruel and insulting' towards slaves, and that made servile respect for the master, as opposed to fear of him, difficult to achieve ([35]). Seneca's apparent distaste for this state of affairs was virtually exceptional ([36]), so it is not surprising that Roman literature is replete with examples of slaves being punished, and by describing merely a few of them it is easy to see what the principal kinds of punishment were, what offences led to them, and what kinds of slaves received them. The unhistorical nature of some of the literary stories again does not deprive them of significance when it is remembered that authors wrote in the belief that their readers would recognise common elements in the master-slave relationship in their works.

Flogging was a widespread punishment for which, it seems, little justification was required. Juvenal shows slaves being flogged by professional employees as a result of their mistress' pique for her husband, and he offers also a scene of a slave-owner standing over his slaves, whip in hand, as they clean the house ([37]). Less sensationally Varro advised that farm-hands should only be beaten by the *uilicus* if words did not achieve the desired effect, but Tacitus refers to slaves being flogged as their owner lay on his deathbed and Ammianus Marcellinus reports that owners in his day might have slaves beaten three hundred times for an offence as trivial as being slow to bring hot water ([38]). In Diodorus' description of servile conditions in the mines in Spain, moreover, beating is a staple ingredient ([39]). The prevalence in the first century of *ergastula* for housing

(33) ATH. 6.265a ; cf. SEN. *Clem.* 1.18.2, *in seruum omnia liceant.*

(34) TAC. *Germ.* 25.2 ; SEN. *Epp.* 47.5. Cf. Ps. PLUT. *De lib. ed.* 12 : physical punishment is fit only for slaves.

(35) SEN. *Epp.* 47.11 ; 17-19.

(36) Cf. however EPICT. *Diss.* 1.13.2, and cf. CREŢIA(1961),373f., MILANI (1972), 222f., and BRUNT (1973), 18f. on Dio Chrysostom ; on Seneca and slavery see MILANI (1972), 212ff. and GRIFFIN (1976), 256ff., and for Roman attitudes towards cruelty in general see LINTOTT (1968), 35ff.

(37) IUV. 6.474ff. ; 14.60f. ; cf. BARBU (1963), 68.

(38) VARRO, *RR.* 1.17.5 ; TAC. *Ann.* 16.19.4 ; AMM. MARC. 28.4.16 ; cf. also PLUT. *Cato* 21.3.

(39) DIOD. SIC. 5.38. In the *Satyricon*, the heroes on entering Trimalchio's house find themselves confronted by a desperate domestic who entreats them to rescue him from a

rural slaves can be assumed from Columella's recommendations on their upkeep and from the elder Pliny's complaints of the low quality of work performed by their inmates [40]. According to Suetonius these men at the beginning of the imperial age were so dangerous at large as brigands that Augustus was compelled to take coercive action against them ; that hints at a problem of control, as too the supposed abolition of the *ergastula* by Hadrian [41]. Detention in these places involved permanent shackling, and some agricultural workers appear to have been regularly kept in chains during the daytime [42]. No small wonder, then, that the threat of being sent to the country as punishment was held over the heads of urban slaves [43], yet shackling was frequent elsewhere as well : Augustus, for example, put in chains a certain Cosmus for having made some insulting remarks, and the penalty was considered mild [44]. Equally, slaves were branded in punishment, for an offence according to Juvenal as slight as stealing a couple of towels [45], and the elder Pliny's reference to the branding of slaves' faces lends credibility to the ruse of Eumolpus in the *Satyricon* whereby the heroes' foreheads were covered with false inscriptions to make authentic their disguise as slaves [46]. Finally, the

steward whose clothes have been stolen, and Trimalchio himself has a slave beaten for bandaging his bruised arm with white instead of purple wool (PETR. *Sat.* 30.7-11 ; 54.4). On Trimalchio's doorpost there was an inscription reading, 'Any slave leaving the house without the master's permission will receive one hundred lashes' (PETR. *Sat.* 28.7) ; cf. COL. *RR.* 11.1.23, servile absence from the farm only under extreme conditions, and for the connection between flight, theft and flogging, HOR. *Epist* 1.16.46f. On incidental allusions to cruelty in literature, cf. HOPKINS (1978), 118.

(40) See above p. 21 ; PLIN. *NH* 18.36 ; cf. 21 ; on the history and meaning of the term *ergastulum* see R. ETIENNE, *Recherches sur l'ergastule* in *Actes du Colloque 1972 sur l'esclavage*, Paris, 1974, 249ff. and J. C. FITZGIBBON, *Ergastula* in *Echos du monde classique / Classical News and Views* 20 (1976), 55ff.

(41) SUET. *Aug.* 32.1 ; *HA Hadr.* 18.10 ; cf. the difficulty of restraining the *pastores* of southern Italy (TAC. *Ann.* 4.27 ; 12.65.1), on the background to which see T. P. WISEMAN, *Viae Anniae* in *PBSR* 32 (1964), 21ff. ; Brunt (1971), 551ff. According to *HA Seu. Alex.* 27.1-3, Severus Alexander wished to have slaves wear distinctive dress to allow easy recognition and to cut down disorder (*ne quis seditiosus esset*). In spite of Hadrian's alleged suppression, the term *ergastulum* appears in Apuleius (*Apol.* 47 ; cf. *Met.* 9.12) as if still in common use.

(42) COL. *RR.* 1.6.3 ; 1.9.4 refer to slaves working in vineyards as the *uincti* or *alligati* ; cf. MART. *Epig.* 9.23 and contrast PLINY (*Epp.* 3.19.7), who avoided chain-gangs, unusually.

(43) HOR. *Sat.* 2.7.118 ; IUV. 8.179f. ; cf. PLAUT. *Bacch.* 365 ; *Asin.* 341f.

(44) SUET. *Aug.* 67.1.

(45) IUV. 14.15ff.

(46) PLIN. *NH* 18.21 ; PETR. *Sat.* 103 ; cf. also MART. *Epig.* 8.75 ; DIO CHRYS. *Or.* 14.19 ;

practice was common of compelling slaves to wear iron collars which bore their owners' names or addresses so that fugitives could be appropriately returned on capture ([47]).

The omnipotence of the master over the slave was such that the way was open not just for the exercise of these, as it were, standard types of physical punishment and treatment, but also for the devising of exceptional acts of cruelty in which sadistic tendencies on the part of some owners stand out clearly. In this respect Roman emperors figure prominently in the literary record. For example, a slave who had stolen a piece of silver plate at a banquet given by Caligula is said, upon detection, to have been handed over at once by the emperor to a *carnifex* : his hands were cut off and hung around his neck, and he was then paraded around the dining hall with a placard giving the reasons for his misfortune ([48]). Such an atrocity cannot be attributed solely to Caligula's possible derangement. Augustus had the legs of a slave named Thallus broken for taking a bribe, while the *paedagogus* and other attendants of his grandson C. Caesar were thrown into a river with weights tied around their necks for having too precipitately anticipated their master's death ([49]). While similar stories surround other emperors ([50]), they are not confined to the imperial house alone. Larcius Macedo represents the type of the cruel master, *superbus alioqui dominus et saeuus* ([51]), whose enormities against slaves there was little to prevent, such as the decision of the infamous Vedius Pollio to feed to his lampreys a boy who had broken a crystal cup ([52]). Seneca portrays a gourmand at dinner surrounded by a retinue of slaves whose slightest murmurs − coughs, sneezes and hiccups − were suppressed with the rod, and Juvenal describes the cruel Rutilus

---

Ovid, *Trist.* 4.1.5 ; *Pont.* 1.6.31. Constantine abolished branding of the face as a criminal penalty, reserving it for hands and legs only ; *CTh.* 9.40.2.

(47) Examples available at *ILS* 8726-8733 ; the practice was not mitigated by Christianity ; cf. G. Sotgiu, *Un collare di schiava rinvenuto in Sardegna* in *Archeologia Classica* 25-26 (1973-74), 688ff. The collars may be one of the stigmatising signs of slavery referred to at Dion. Hal. 4.14.4.

(48) Suet. *Cal.* 32.2.

(49) Suet. *Aug.* 57.1-2.

(50) Hadrian is said to have stabbed a slave in the eye with a stylus in a fit of anger (Galen 5.17-18, Kühn) ; Macrinus had a particular reputation for flogging slaves (*HA Macr.* 13.3) ; and Valentinian killed off slaves in Germany to eliminate a security threat (Amm. Marc. 29.4.4.) ; cf. also *HA Hadr.* 21.3.

(51) Plin. *Epp.* 3.14.1 ; cf. Petr. *Sat.* 107.4, *saeui quoque implacabilesque domini* ; Amm. Marc. 25.4.2, *rabiosus ... dominus et crudelis*.

(52) Sen. *Ira* 3.40.2 ; cf. *Clem.* 1.18.2 ; Dio 54.23.1-4 ; Plin. *NH* 9.77.

delighting in the infliction on his slaves of flogging, branding and incarceration ([53]).

It is thus indisputable that physical coercion from the owner played a large part in servile life in one way or another and that subjection to brutality was a basic component of slavery. It may readily be allowed that some of the literary stories referred to attracted the attention of writers because they were extreme examples of cruelty ; and it was of course the case that outrages were perceived and not necessarily condoned : 'If one were to crucify a slave who, when bidden to take away a dish, has greedily licked up the half-eaten fish and its sauce, now cold, sane men would call him more insane than Labeo,' Horace wrote, and again, 'If you were to take to pelting stones ... at your own slaves, for whom you've paid in cash, all would hoot at you as mad' ([54]). But any thought that the anecdotal nature of the literary evidence makes that evidence totally suspect is shattered by the testimony of an inscription from Puteoli, which gives details of the duties of a public official (*manceps*) in charge of local burials, duties which included the torture and execution of slaves. If a private citizen wished to punish a slave (male or female), he could on payment of a fee have public facilities (*crux, patibulum, uerberatores*) put at his disposal, the *manceps* having to see that all the necessary apparatus was provided. Local officials could have slaves tortured free of charge, and again the *manceps* had to ensure availability of instruments and personnel, and to take care subsequently of the removal of corpses ([55]). The point is that there was no real restraint on the slave-owner, other than his own temperament or conscience, to prevent outrage or extremity if circumstance led to it : any slave who offended his owner could expect not only punishment but severe punishment, the penalty apparently often exceeding the transgression, especially in cases of sheer accidents. The threat of punishment always overhung servile activities and since

(53) Sen. *Epp*. 47.2-3 ; Iuv. 14.15ff.

(54) Hor. *Sat*. 1.3.80-82 ; 2.3.128-130, Loeb translation. While there are notorious instances of brutality in the literary record, the most common forms of punishment were perhaps not such as to destroy the slave property. Limits on masters' severity must have been imposed by the realisation that frequent excessive punishment acted against their own best economic interests ; cf. Burford (1972), 42f. Men such as Vedius Pollio and Larcius Macedo were doubtless extreme.

(55) *AE* 1971 no. 88, II 8-14 ; cf. Lucio Bove, *Due inscrizione da Pozzuoli e Cuma* in *Labeo* 13 (1967), 22ff. ; Francesco de Martino, *I "supplicia" dell'inscrizione di Pozzuoli* in *Labeo* 21 (1975), 210ff. ; Finley (1980), 95.

penalties could be inflicted either by the owner or an underling there was often more than one person to fear. While it should not be thought that all slaves in Roman society were being physically violated all the time, it is nevertheless true that all slaves were under the constant pressure of exposure to punishment and that such pressure formed another aspect of the servile mentality [56].

Moreover, even from the limited amount of material considered so far, it is clear, and requires stress, that servile distinctions of status, function, age or sex gave no protection against arbitrary punishment. It may be an accident of the sources that more details are preserved on the harsh treatment of domestic than other slaves : Juvenal's evidence contains references to a woolmaid, a litter-bearer, a maidservant, and indeed the full domestic household ; Martial adds a hairdresser and a cook [57] ; Caligula's slave must have been a waiter ; Thallus was obviously some kind of secretary. Agricultural and mining slaves were certainly exposed to the same climate of violence and even children were not spared, but urban domestics were more visible to their owners than their rural counterparts and they were thus at a particular disadvantage as far as the infliction of punishment was concerned. In view of their relative advantages in the areas of creating families and achieving manumission, this point is valuable for offsetting the common belief that the conditions of urban slaves were always more favourable than those of slaves elsewhere.

In what ways could the slave find protection against arbitrary cruelty from the master ? As seen already, excess led at times to slaves' own physical retaliation against their owners, though this must have been an extremely dangerous undertaking. But there were other means, notably through the law, which were at least theoretically available to slaves, mechanisms whose purpose was perhaps to prevent the possibility of physical danger and injury to owners from retaliating slaves. At Rome it was the responsibility of the city prefect (*praefectus urbi*) to hear slaves' complaints of cruel treatment, perhaps from the inception of the office under Augustus and certainly soon thereafter [58]. In the provinces the

(56) For the relationship between physical punishment and the absence of servile *dignitas* see Lintott (1968), 46.

(57) MART. *Epig.* 2.66 ; 8.23.

(58) *Dig.* 1.12.1.1 ; 8 ; SEN. *Ben.* 3.22.3 ; cf. BELLEN (1971), 66ff. ; GRIFFIN (1976), 269f. ; (cf. 460f.).

same function was filled by the governor ([59]). Yet it is questionable how often, from the servile point of view, these procedures were successfully applied. Roman law as a whole favoured the interests of the elite over those of the lower social orders ([60]) and it might thus be thought unlikely that slave-owning officials would have been genuinely open and impartial to slaves who appeared before them. A slave who wished to seek legal redress had to face the problem of the official's availability, which as in the case of obtaining formal manumission must always have been unpredictable. At Rome there appears to have been a special site where the city prefect could be found, though how often is not known, while in the provinces the limiting conditions of the circuit tour again prevailed ([61]). And the slave's very decision to seek help from the authorities is likely to have involved desperate action on his part before access to officials was even gained : since the slave-owner could to some degree control the slave's movements ([62]), and cannot be expected usually to have given permission to leave the household or estate for complaints to be made against himself, the slave was compelled to abscond and to take refuge often at a place of asylum ([63]). This is not to say that the slave's position was hopeless, but it is to emphasise the risks and difficulties which attended appeal ([64]).

In the early imperial age the right of asylum, originally a Greek rather than Roman convention, came to be associated with temples and representations of the emperor both at Rome and in the provinces ([65]). Under Tiberius, sanctuary before a statue of Augustus was claimed in Crete ; it had become a capital offence to beat a slave near such a statue ;

(59) GAIUS, *Inst.* 1.53 ; *Dig.* 1.6.2 ; *Instit.* 1.8.2 ; this evidence refers to rulings of the emperor Antoninus Pius, but the governor was probably hearing slaves' appeals earlier since rights of asylum (see below) were already in existence.

(60) GARNSEY (1970), passim. ; cf. also *Legal Privilege in the Roman Empire* in M. I. Finley, ed., *Studies in Ancient Society*, London, 1974, 141ff.

(61) *Dig.* 1.12.1.1 with BELLEN (1971), 66f. ; above, pp. 101ff. JONKERS (1934), 243 perhaps overestimates the ease with which complaints were made.

(62) Cf. COL. *RR*. 11.1.23.

(63) He did not thereby become a fugitive, however, technically at least ; *Dig.* 21.1.17.12.

(64) According to *HA Pert.* 9.10, slaves who had brought false charges (*calumniae*) against their masters were crucified by Pertinax ; how the *calumniae* were established is not made clear by the text.

(65) See for example DIO 47.19.2 ; TAC. *Ann.* 3.36 (cf. 3.60) ; SUET. *Aug.* 17.5 ; SEN. *Clem.* 1.18.2 ; BELLEN (1971), 64ff. ; St. WEINSTOCK, *Divus Julius*, Oxford, 1971, 242f. ; cf. DAUBE (1972), 57f. ; HOPKINS (1978), 221ff.

and even statues of the living emperor were deemed to afford protection [66]. Among those who could legitimately draw on the safety of asylum were slaves who had complaints against their owners, protection which was certainly drawn upon [67]. Even so it is not altogether clear whether a fair hearing of the complaints followed : in circumstances admittedly exceptional, right of asylum was simply violated when Augustus executed the sons of M. Antonius and his wife Fulvia, who had taken refuge at a statue of the deified Julius [68]. Nor is it safe to assume that access to an official was always automatic once asylum had been sought : refuge at a busy time of day in order to compel attention and a hearing, when public awareness of the situation was intense, was urged to the elder Agrippina and Nero Caesar under harassment from Sejanus again in Tiberius' reign [69]. The younger Pliny dealt with a fugitive in Bithynia who had sought refuge before a statue of Trajan, but it should be noted that the slave had earlier appeared before other, presumably municipal, magistrates [70], a circumstance which may at other times have hindered access to the governor's tribunal. All in all the frequency with which slave suppliants were able to come before Roman magistrates and to be heard sympathetically cannot be determined, but it is doubtful that the law and reality often coincided equitably. And even in the event of a successful hearing the benefit which accrued to the slave was no more than sale to a new owner, to judge from a ruling of Antoninus Pius [71], whereby the slave became exposed to new possibilities of abuse.

Again in theory and to some extent in practice the emperor himself was available to slaves for appeal, as he was to other members of society. Petitions were received from slaves and emperors gave responses, but as seen earlier factors of time, distance, cost and imperial temperament meant that this source of redress was unusual for slaves rather than a common occurrence [72]. Moreover, the majority of attested imperial responses to servile petitions concern questions of slaves' status and not

---

(66) TAC. *Ann*. 3.63 ; SUET. *Tib*. 58 ; (cf. PLIN. *Epp*. 10.74).

(67) PLIN. *Epp*. 10.74, and legal texts cited in n. 59. On asylum as protection against sexual abuse see TREGGIARI (1979b), 192.

(68) SUET. *Aug*. 17.5.

(69) TAC. *Ann*. 4.67.

(70) PLIN. *Epp*. 10.74.1.

(71) *Dig*. 1.6.2 ; cf. BELLEN (1971), 66ff. ; GRIFFIN (1976), 269f. ; WILLIAMS (1976), 76f.

(72) See above, pp. 102f. with references.

questions of abuse or maltreatment [73]. On the other hand Hadrian is known to have relegated for five years a woman who had harmed her maidservants (*ancillae*) [74] ; yet the details of the episode – the precise nature of the charges and how the emperor came to be involved – are beyond recovery. An incident between Augustus and Vedius Pollio, however, suggests that imperial intervention could be totally fortuitous, for Augustus, while at dinner with Vedius Pollio, is reported to have saved from the man-eating fish a slave who made a timely appeal to him, and then to have rebuked the slave's owner [75]. To say the least Augustus' location was highly convenient for this particular individual and there can have been few other slaves fortunate enough to obtain the emperor's clemency in this fashion at such personally critical moments.

The conclusion follows, therefore, that a significant dichotomy existed between the potential of legal relief for slaves who had unduly suffered from their owners and the realisation of that potential, an imbalance which operated firmly in the interests of slave-owners and against those of slaves : according to a ruling of Constantine a slave-owner whose slave had died after punishment was not himself subject to a penalty unless the slave's punishment had been immoderate [76]. Yet this view, which many might regard as overly cynical, would seem to be vitiated by the knowledge that in the imperial period a series of laws was enacted which ostensibly brought about a great improvement of servile conditions. Whereas in technical terms the master's power over his slaves, including the power of life and death, remained constant, in actuality a number of legal developments had the effect of bringing slaves more and more under the control of the state [77]. For instance, the slave-owner's ability to consign slaves to wild beasts in the arena was abolished (the *lex Petronia*) : sick slaves who were abandoned by their owners but who subsequently recovered were not returned to their owners but were set free ; the master

---

(73) See the items collected in Piganiol (1958).

(74) *Dig.* 1.6.2 ; *Coll.* 3.3.4.

(75) Sen. *Ira* 3.40.2 ; cf. *Clem.* 1.18.2 ; Dio 54.23.1-4 ; Plin. *NH* 9.77 seems to equate the feeding to fish with the penalty of *bestiae*. On Pollio see R. Syme, *Who was Vedius Pollio* ? in *JRS* 51 (1961), 23ff. = *Roman Papers*, Oxford, 1979, II 518ff. Is it possible that the episode between Pollio and Augustus influenced the creation of the office of *praefectus urbi* ?

(76) *CJ* 9.14.1. The loophole for the master is obvious.

(77) See in general Buckland (1908), 36ff. ; Westermann (1955), 114f. ; Griffin (1976), 268f.

who killed a slave became subject to trial for homicide, and the master was required to give up a slave proved to have suffered excessive brutality. Castration of slaves was also banned [78].

The usual interpretation of this legislation is that it reflects the growth of a humanitarian concern for slaves in the imperial age [79], a notion which, although perhaps containing some truth, is beyond proof and inconsistent with what can be determined of actual practice as seen so far. It could be said that protection against cruelty to slaves was given more attention than in the past by the various emperors who were responsible for rulings ; but pronouncements were not necessarily matched by compliance, and not only do the limitations already described on the slave's capacity to secure redress have to be kept in mind here, but the degree of amelioration of the slave's conditions contained in the law can be shown to have been not really all that great. Claudius' grant of freedom to abandoned sick slaves who recovered their health is the only certain case in which genuine protection against future abuse and violence can be allowed : freedom permitted change because subjection to the will of a slave-owner was fully eradicated, though it should be noted that the slave was not given full freedom but only Junian status [80]. But in the ban, established by the *lex Petronia*, on masters arbitrarily assigning slaves to the wild beasts of the amphitheatre, the law continued to uphold that penalty if the slave-owner were able to prove just cause against his slave [81], a rather obvious loophole. And given an inferable identification of social status and general interest between owner and magistrate, it may be doubted that the latter frequently pronounced in favour of the slave in cases of this sort. At any rate, the *lex Petronia* did nothing to diminish the severity of other forms of physical punishment, nor did the laws on homicide and castration, and again, significantly, in cases where a slave was able to show excessive cruelty – which must have been difficult since the right of the master not to be accused by his own slave was preserved [82] – the law allowed only for his sale to a new owner, the

---

(78) *Dig.* 48.8.11.1-2 ; 18.1.42 ; 40.8.2 ; 1.6.1.2 ; SUET. *Claud.* 25.2 ; GAIUS, *Inst.* 1.53 ; *Instit.* 1.8.2 ; cf. *HA Hadr.* 18.7 ; for castration see below, pp. 128f.

(79) E.g., WESTERMANN (1955), 116f. ; BURFORD (1972), 50 ; contrast GRIFFIN (1976), 268f.

(80) BUCKLAND (1908), 37. Cf., however, TERT. *Apol.* 39. 6.

(81) *Dig.* 48.8.11.2, *iusta querella*.

(82) *Dig.* 1.12.8, *nisi ex causis receptis*.

value of which for future protection can hardly be said to have been great [83].

The law on castration requires special attention because it illustrates particularly well the problems of enforcement which can be presumed to have applied to all the 'ameliorative' legislation, and because it shows how insubstantial improvement really was. Within roughly fifty years around the turn of the first and second centuries castration was legislated against on three occasions : Domitian first forbade castration of slaves on Roman soil ; Nerva then followed suit, fixing the penalty at *publicatio* of half the guilty party's estate ; and in a rescript to a Spanish governor Hadrian finally made offenders liable to the *lex Cornelia de sicariis et ueneficiis* [84]. The action of Nerva implies that Domitian's original order had had little effect, and Hadrian's ruling implies the same for Nerva's law, which indeed is clear from the banishment of an offender for five years by the Spanish governor to whom Hadrian wrote [85], as well as from allusions, which belong after Domitian's death, to the castration of slave boys in Juvenal's poems [86]. Although the homosexual market for eunuchs was supplied in part by imports from beyond the borders of the Roman Empire [87], it seems implausible to believe that castration within the borders was impeded by Hadrian's ruling any more than by those of his predecessors. The slave-dealer who castrated boys was not as exposed to the possibility of future retaliation as the cruel master who repeatedly abused his slaves, because he disposed of his property relatively quickly (and at a profit) and did not have to worry over the problem of a lengthy relationship with the slaves he sold. Impressive evidence is available from late antiquity to show the ubiquity of eunuchs in the Empire [88], and that

---

(83) *Dig.* 1.6.2 ; cf. n. 71. According to *HA Hadr.* 18.8 ; 10, Hadrian abolished *ergastula*, but unsuccessfully (above, n. 41 ; cf. BUCKLAND (1908), 37 n. 4), and banned the sale of female and male slaves to pimps and gladiatorial entrepreneurs respectively, but with the proviso, *causa non praestita* ; the action did nothing to stop slave prostitution ; cf., e.g., *CTh.* 15.8.1. The information of *HA Hadr.* 18 is reliable (see Richard BAUMANN, *Legislation in the Historia Augusta* in *ZSS Rom. Abt.* 94 (1977), 43ff. at pp. 45ff.), but a distinction still persists between passage and enforcement of legislation.

(84) SUET. *Dom.* 7 ; Dio 67.2.3 ; 68.2.3 ; MART. *Epig.* 2.60 ; AMM. MARC. 18.4.5 ; *Dig.* 48.8.4.1-2 ; 48.8.5-6 ; *Paul. Sent.* 5.23.13.

(85) *Dig.* 48.8.4.1.

(86) IUV. 6.373, which belongs near the transition from Trajan to Hadrian ; see E. COURTNEY, *A Commentary on the Satires of Juvenal*, London, 1980, 1 ; cf. also R. SYME, *Juvenal, Pliny, Tacitus* in *AJP* 100 (1979), 250ff.

(87) HOPKINS (1978), 172ff.

(88) HOPKINS (1978), 172ff.

suggests that earlier legislation against castration had simply become a dead letter. The ability of the slave to set in motion the legal machinery of redress, the chances of detection, trial and punishment were not great enough to restrict the practice of castration as long as it was profitable, and to that extent servile conditions did not improve.

What may have been genuinely compassionate motivations on the part of the individual emperors responsible for legislation on slavery should not be unnecessarily impugned. But as already seen humanitarianism does not have a great bearing on the master-slave relationship in Roman society as a whole, and improvement of servile conditions for its own sake may not have been the real or only cause of the various enactments to which reference has been made. In a rescript to a provincial governor handed down by Antoninus Pius, obedience (obsequium) was ordered in slaves and mild treatment of them by their masters commanded, under the threat of the governor's intervention, 'in case greater danger should arise' ([89]). This suggests that ameliorative legislation was intended less to afford protection to slaves than to restrain the owner from excess for the sake of maintaining order among the servile population, eventually to the benefit of the master, a view consistent with the fears of slave resistance seen earlier, the overall tendency of Roman law to favour higher social interests, and no more than minimal literary evidence from the imperial period of true humanitarian concern for slaves ([90]). The arbitrary physical abuse of slaves cannot be said to have been dramatically alleviated by legislation of an improving kind.

Under Roman law slaves were subject to criminal penalties just as other segments of the population, and in this respect they were not exposed to a particular form of treatment which was not experienced by other social groups as well. The inherent bias of the Roman legal system meant, however, that lower social categories were discriminated against as far as the application of punishment was concerned ([91]), and slaves, as the lowest category of all, suffered the most severe types of criminal penalty : 'Our ancestors have in every penalty punished slaves more

(89) *Coll.* 3.3.5-6, *ne quid tumultuosius contra accidat* ; cf. WILLIAMS (1976), 77.

(90) Cf. BRUNT (1973), 18 on Stoic philosophers, 'Of course Stoics urged masters to treat their slaves justly and kindly ... But one constantly feels that Stoics were concerned rather with the moral evil involved in injustice than with the sufferings of the slaves'.

(91) Cf. GARNSEY (1970), 121 ; 152.

severely than free men' so a passage from the *Digest* states [92]. Thus, for example, conviction under the *lex Cornelia de falsis* brought deportation for a free person but death for a slave [93]; and in the regulations governing the mines at Vipasca in Spain, the crime of stealing ore was punishable by a fine of HS1,000, though 'If a person who steals ore is a slave, the procurator shall have him beaten and shall sell him on the condition that he shall be kept in chains for ever and that he shall not remain in any mining camps or mining district' [94]. Slaves were consequently exposed to stronger pressures by the criminal legal system, pressures which remained constant over time since criminal liability itself remained constant.

Of course slaves were not unique in receiving harsh penalties. In the army the ancient punishment of decimation was still at times practised in the imperial period, and individual miscreants were flogged, occasionally even executed, or else subjected to other ignominious penalties [95]. Josephus was able to comment upon the element of fear in military training and its connection with military discipline [96], a fitting analogy for the relationship between fear and servile discipline. Moreover, a distinct trend can be perceived under the early Empire towards the infliction of what traditionally had been servile punishments only (*seruilia supplicia*) to the broad social group that came to be classified as *humiliores* [97]. It may be in consequence that before the law slaves gradually became less and less of a distinct group, and certainly the simple division between slave and free is of no use for a discussion of criminal

---

(92) *Dig.* 48.19.28.16, *maiores nostri in omni supplicio seuerius seruos quam liberos ... punierunt.*

(93) *Instit.* 4.8.17.

(94) *FIRA*² III no. 104, translation from A. C. JOHNSON, P. R. COLEMAN-NORTON, F. C. BOURNE, *The Corpus of Roman Law* II, Austin, 1961, no. 233. Cato executed slaves after trial, PLUT. *Cato* 21.4.

(95) See G. R. WATSON, *The Roman Soldier*, London, 1969, 117ff. for details.

(96) Jos. *BJ* 3.102-104, 'By their military exercises the Romans instil into their soldiers fortitude not only of body but also of soul ; fear, too, plays its part in their training. For they have laws which punish with death not merely desertion of the ranks, but even a slight neglect of duty ; and their generals are held in even greater awe than the laws. For the high honours with which they reward the brave prevent the offenders whom they punish from regarding themselves as treated cruelly. This perfect discipline makes the army an ornament of peace-time and in war welds the whole into a single body' ; (Loeb translation).

(97) P. D. A. GARNSEY, *Why Penalties Become Harsher : the Roman Case, Late Republic to Fourth-Century Empire* in *Natural Law Forum* 13 (1968), 141ff.

penalties ([98]). But while the criminal treatment of slaves should not be seen outside the context of criminal penalties as a whole, military discipline and the depression of *humiliores* are largely irrelevant for present purposes because these matters did not affect the impact on actual servile expectations as far as the criminal law was concerned : slaves knew at all stages of imperial history that criminal conviction entailed extreme physical suffering for them.

The death penalty was used no more than sparingly for upper-class offenders, with the exception of cases of treason (*maiestas*), and simple decapitation, or even the alternative of voluntary exile, was then the mode of punishment. In strong contrast persons of low social rank, including slaves, were subject to punishment by death for many offences and in several forms : burning alive (*crematio*), crucifixion (*crux*), and exposure to wild animals in the amphitheatre (*bestiae*) ([99]).

According to Callistratus *crematio* was the penalty for slaves who had conspired against their owners, and presumably it was applied against the households of the men known from literary sources to have been attacked in the first and early second centuries, L. Pedanius Secundus, Larcius Macedo and Afranius Dexter, and indeed against the whole households – in the Pedanius Secundus affair, a total number of four hundred slaves, according to Tacitus, including women and children – not simply those who had committed the assaults ([100]). In situations such as these the law exempted from punishment slaves whose connivance was logically impossible, but it showed no other tendency towards mildness ([101]). Consequently many slaves who even contemplated an act of violence against their owners must have been well aware that action would have opened not only themselves to the possibility of grim execution but also friends and family members in their various households. This danger might then well account for the relative shortage of recorded attacks by slaves on their owners if the literary record is indeed a genuine reflection of reality.

Death by crucifixion is well-attested in the central periods of Roman history ([102]). Its use by the triumvir M. Crassus to punish the slave rebels

(98) Cf. GARNSEY (1970), 103ff.
(99) GARNSEY (1970), 105ff. ; 111ff.
(100) *Dig.* 48.19.28.11, *igni cremantur* ; TAC. *Ann.* 14.43.4 ; 45.1.
(101) BUCKLAND (1908), 95 ; SHERWIN-WHITE (1966), 463.
(102) See M. HENGEL, *Crucifixion in the Ancient World*, Philadelphia, 1977, 51ff. ; GARNSEY (1970), 127.

who had followd Spartacus ([103]) is perhaps comprehensible, a drastic end
to a drastic episode, but far lesser crimes than armed rebellion drew the
punishment. Caligula is said to have crucified an ex-slave who knew of
his role in Tiberius' death ; Domitian crucified the secretaries of
Hermogenes of Tarsus for having transcribed their master's questionable
history ; and Severus Alexander supposedly crucified a eunuch for
venality ([104]). In Trimalchio's gazette the crucifixion of a slave named
Mithradates is announced following his slander of Trimalchio, while in
Juvenal crucifixion is made to appear the prerogative of the master
without any semblance of a trial at all, or even of a crime ([105]). It is a
reasonable supposition that the execution of slaves in the area on the
Esquiline at Rome which was specially reserved for the punishment of
slaves was a common sight ([106]).

Condemnation to wild beasts in the amphitheatre must have entailed an
even more grisly form of execution. Again in Petronius a realistic detail
emerges in the record of the sentencing of a slave to *bestiae* for having
committed adultery with a freeborn woman ([107]). But perhaps the most
vivid accounts of this penalty appear in the records of early Christian
martyrdoms, which included both slaves and free persons ([108]). Thus a
female slave Blandina, one of a group of Christians martyred at
Lugdunum in the reign of Marcus Aurelius, was first exposed to animals
in the local amphitheatre, then hung on a stake as bait, scourged and
exposed to animals a second time, put on a burning seat and tied up in a
net before a third and final exposure, which resulted in her death ([109]).
Blandina's treatment is known from a source highly sympathetic to her
and Christians of servile status were not the only ones to be executed in
this manner ([110]). But there seems little cause to doubt the details of

---

(103) App. *BC* 1.120.

(104) Suet. *Cal.* 12.2 ; *Dom.* 10.1 ; *HA Seu. Alex.* 23.8.

(105) Petr. *Sat.* 53.3 ; Iuv. 6.219ff.

(106) Tac. *Ann.* 15.60.2 ; cf. Platner, Ashby (1929), s.v. 'Sessorium'.

(107) Petr. *Sat.* 45. Note that Aurelian allegedly punished with death a maidservant
who had committed adultery with a fellow slave ; *HA Aur.* 49.5.

(108) Evidence collected in H. Musurillo, *The Acts of the Christian Martyrs*, Oxford,
1972. The literature on martyrology is of course immense, but for the background see
especially W. H. C. Frend, *Martyrdom and Persecution in the Early Church*, Oxford,
1965.

(109) *Mart. Lug.* (1) 36 ; 41 ; 56 (Musurillo) ; cf. also the slave Felicitas, *Mart. Lug.* (1)
18 (Musurillo).

(110) See Garnsey (1970), 129ff. for other examples. The point, again, is that while
bestiae came to be used against non-servile groups, for slaves it remained a constant form

Blandina's death, and her execution may serve as a paradigm for the penalty of *bestiae* whether or not in a Christian context.

The prospect of capital punishment cannot have affected the quality of servile life in the same way as that of capricious punishment from the individual slave-owner : in contemplating or planning a crime slaves were able to foresee the possible result of personal physical suffering, but this was a risk open to calculation. In one respect, however, namely with regard to torture, the law was arbitrary, and although in the imperial period the use of torture to extract evidence for criminal proceedings from free persons is documented, for slaves it was traditional and their liability again remained constant and without variation [111]. Even so, the amount of psychological pressure exercised by the prospect of torture varied among slaves in relation to their proximity to their owners. Those who formed part of their owner's retinue, accompanying him wherever he went, or those who attended in some other personal capacity – for example, waiters, dressers, barbers – were much better situated for picking up incriminating information than non-domestics. The domestic staffs of Roman senators, men directly engaged in politics, were especially prone to torture at moments of conspiracy, real or imagined, against the emperor. And whereas slaves were theoretically prevented by the law from being tortured to provide evidence against their owners, devices were concocted to circumvent the law, as when, under Tiberius, the slaves of C. Iunius Silanus were compulsorily sold during his trial so that they could be appropriately interrogated [112]. In spite of the availability of torture for all slaves, therefore, once more the better living conditions of domestic slaves in prominent urban households were offset by the increased likelihood of physical abuse in a legally institutionalised form.

The severity and constancy of servile criminal penalties are quite clearly consistent with attitudes towards slaves revealed by methods of private correction, but in degree they often exceeded what might be considered standard forms of private punishment. Part of the explanation for this must lie in the nature of the social status of the slave criminal, for while an upper class offender could find his social rank impaired on criminal

of execution. Christian slaves could be confronted with the expectation of *bestiae* on a double count eventually.

(111) GARNSEY (1970), 141ff.

(112) BUCKLAND (1908), 88 ; TAC. *Ann.* 2.30.3 ; cf. VAL. MAX. 6.8.1. For slaves as betrayers of their masters' secrets cf. IUV. 9.102ff. ; and for some cases of torture see SUET. *Aug.* 19.2 ; *Galba* 10.5 ; TAC. *Ann.* 1.23.3 ; 3.14.3 ; 3.50.1 ; 4.29 ; 14.60.4.

conviction, through the loss of citizenship or property as a sequel to exile [113], the slave, as a member of society with no technical rights or privileges, could not suffer any reduction of his status at all. Extreme physical punishment of the slave was thus the only avenue open to the law, which exhibited no moral qualms about the infliction of brutality on slaves [114]. In addition, it could be believed that the anticipation by slaves of severe physical punishment had a deterrent effect upon them : Horace wrote that fear of penalty restrained the slave from crime and C. Cassius, in his speech in the senate after Pedanius Secundus' murder, referred to the effect of 'exemplary punishment' on the servile population [115]. In the view of Epictetus the suffering which resulted from punishment meant that slaves did not commit the same mistake twice [116]. Harsh penalties were prescribed and upheld by the law, therefore, because they afforded the most basic means of containing slaves and of eliciting subordination among them, or, in other words, of achieving *disciplina* [117]. Although individual masters came to lose certain formal prerogatives under the Empire with regard to the indiscriminate punishment of slaves, the conditions of the latter did not significantly improve because the law, subsuming to itself more and more of the master's role, retained and perpetuated physical penalties as harsh as anything seen in the private sector. The intent of the law above all was to intimidate slaves into a state of passivity and acquiescence.

One of the most unusual ways in which violence manifested itself in servile life was that of a slave himself being required to commit a violent act at the instigation of his owner or some other member of free society. The emperor Nero, for example, ordered the death by drowning of his

(113) Cf. GARNSEY (1970), 112.

(114) In view of the maintenance of torture and the forms of execution mentioned above, as well as their extension to *humiliores* at large, the ameliorative slave legislation discussed earlier cannot jeopardise this statement.

(115) HOR. *Epist.* 1.16.53 ; TAC. *Ann.* 14.44.4.

(116) EPICT. *Diss.* 3.25.9-10 ; note also 1.29.59.

(117) See TAC. *Germ.* 25.2 on the connection between punishment and *disciplina* and *seueritas* ; cf. above p. 130 (military discipline). The dividing line between the needs of *disciplina* and the satisfaction of sadistic impulses could be very narrow : Aurelian is said to have had criminal slaves executed in his own presence either to keep up discipline or else to accommodate a lust for cruelty ; *HA Aur.* 49.3-4 ; cf. also PLAUT. *Capt.* 752-753, *ego illis captiuis aliis documentum dabo, ne tale quisquam facinus incipere audeat.* There is much on the need of violence to extract work from slaves in Ballio's speech at PLAUT. *Pseud.* 133ff., and the presentation of a genuine point of view is not to be doubted despite the comic context.

stepson Rufrius Crispinus through the agency of Crispinus' slaves, but assistance in suicide was perhaps more to be expected, as when C. Iunius Silanus asked his slaves to despatch him after his trial [118]. Such assistance was considered by the slave-owner to be an obligation of the slave, an act indeed of obedience to the master's will (*obsequium*) [119]. Examples in the literary record of slaves being manipulated to commit unsavoury acts usually allude to their corruptible nature : slaves by definition, as it were, were so base that they could easily be enticed by their owners to carry out any number of atrocities [120]. Such representation, however, conceals the tension which individuals must have encountered and experienced when confronted by the demand to perform. It might readily be suspected that there was always a certain type of slave to whom such demands came only too willingly, since the use of force under sanction, against any free member of society, would have had a certain inherent attraction. But it must nonetheless be recognised that for others the demands of loyalty and obedience could be stretched unbearably, because their choice lay between a violent act committed out of dutifulness but which might have entailed moral or physical problems on one hand, and a refusal to act which automatically exposed them on the other hand to their owners' anger and reprisal. Whether this was the actual dilemma in which some slaves periodically found themselves, the slave as an agent of violence remains over time a fixed element in literary sources and to that extent the expectation of direct violence in servile life was a condition of life itself [121].

The same is true of course from all the forms of abuse and punishment which have been described so far, as well as such a totally unpredictable eventuality as being kidnapped [122]. There was much of which to be afraid, and an equation between fear and compliance is consequently not

(118) SUET. *Nero* 35.5 ; TAC. *Ann*. 2.31.1-2.

(119) PLIN. *Epp*. 8.14.12. According to the law, however, the slave was supposed to prevent his owner's suicide if at all possible ; *Dig*. 29.5.1.18 ; 22. For other cases of suicide, *HA Hadr*. 24.8 ; TAC. *Ann*. 16.15.4.

(120) On slave corruption see above, pp. 26ff.

(121) See for example TAC. *Ann*. 2.80.2 ; 13.47.4 ; 14.61.3 ; *Hist*. 1.33 ; 2.68 ; 3.64. A slave required to commit a violent act could of course disobey and use his ingenuity to conceal the fact. A story is told of a bath attendant who, on being consigned to the furnace by the young Commodus for having drawn too cool a bath, was rescued from his fate by the slave entrusted to carry out the execution. The latter substituted a sheepskin for the intended victim in the furnace ; *HA Comm*. 1.9.

(122) For cases of abduction, *P. Oxy*. 283 (45) ; *P. Oxy*. 1120 (third century).

difficult to posit. Unfortunately the absence of a real slave literature makes it exceedingly hazardous to estimate the psychological impact (upon individual slaves) of the climate of fear in which they lived, for here even the evidence of sepulchral inscriptions is of no value. The most suggestive material comes from Plautus, dangerous to rely on wholeheartedly by definition, but nonetheless of some value. In *Amphitryon*, for example, there is a long scene between the slave Sosia and Mercury (who has assumed Sosia's identity), the comedy of which depends on the slave being duped by the god. Whatever the contrived or even derivative nature of the encounter, it seems significant that the scene depends for its effect on Sosia being filled with fear of Mercury who at first threatens and finally delivers to the slave a sound thrashing ; the language of fear and beating is unmistakable [123]. In *Pseudolus* the slave Harpax gives a disquisition on how the good slave should conduct himself, namely by maintaining attention to duty even when the master is absent, an attitude which is governed by the slave's fear of his owner [124]. Similarly, Strobilus in *Aulularia* states that utter devotion to and unquestioning obedience of his master is motivated by the desire to avoid physical punishment [125]. The product of this attitude, in the words of Phaniscus in *Mostellaria*, is that 'Slaves who fear a beating, even when they have no cause to fear, are usually their masters' most useful slaves' [126]. Once all allowance is made for comic exaggeration and irony in the plays which provide this material, it seems inconceivable that they are not grounded on true servile fears of slave-owners, fears which continued across time as long as slavery persisted in the Roman world. The fear which the prospect of torture could elicit is illustrated in Eusebius' account of the Christian persecution in which Blandina died, when slaves faced with the danger of tortures they had seen already applied to their Christian owners were prepared to make false accusations against the latter in order to save themselves [127]. Likewise, Epictetus' comments on fugitives' alarms in the theatre on mention of the word 'master' strike a realistic note [128]. The accounts are credible ; the fears of suffering comprehensible.

(123) Plaut. *Amph.* 291ff.
(124) Plaut. *Pseud.* 1103ff.
(125) Plaut. *Aul.* 587ff.
(126) Plaut. *Most.* 859ff.
(127) Euseb. *HE* 5.1.14.
(128) Epict. *Diss.* 1.29.59.

The conditions of life which produced fear of their owners in slaves were thus numerous and all-embracing. The exploitable nature of slaves as commodities led to personal humiliation, notably at the hands of slave-dealers, and their subjection to sexual abuse by their owners led to a similar degradation. The impression is firm that physical punishments meted out to slaves by their owners were consistently brutal, showed little change in the course of time, and were not altered by any distinctions of status among the servile population as a whole. The Roman legal system contained the means by which slaves might seek redress against harsh treatment, yet a strong distinction existed between the theory of the law and its application in real circumstances, because slaves who wished to complain of cruelty were confronted by a string of practical difficulties inimical to their impartial treatment, and because the law contained loopholes detrimental to their interests. The state, as represented by the law, did little to improve servile conditions in the imperial period, but arrogated to itself certain prerogatives which had previously belonged exclusively to slave-owners. By penalties handed down against them, the law thus institutionalised the use of violence against slaves, who were persistently discriminated against because of their very status.

Moreover, Roman slave-owners understood well the deterrent value of punishment and the fact that force could be used to control subordinates when other tactics of manipulation failed or were lacking. Force was deliberately exploited to aid the repression of the slave classes. The overall result was that the frequent recourse to physical coercion produced pain and hardship in the lives of countless slaves over successive generations of which virtually nothing is heard in conventional sources. Slaves were never in a position to predict when the wrath of an owner would descend upon them and their lives were thus conditioned by this perennial fear of physical abuse and maltreatment. Within that element of fear lay owners' capacity for the permanent control of their slaves.

EPILOGUE

CONTROL

Among the forms of compulsory labour which emerged in classical antiquity, chattel slavery ranked at the bottom of the scale insofar as the sheer rightlessness of slaves and masters' expectations of their total obedience to authority were concerned [1]. Chattel slavery was an extreme type of compulsory labour. From this conceptual standpoint it would be tempting to assume that slave-owners were able to control their slaves, to secure loyalty and to extract work from them, with relative ease [2] ; for it was certainly in the nature of slavery in the Roman world that the master had absolute authority over the slave, who was always a dependent being, and that the conditions under which the slave spent his life were laid down either by the owner or else the state, in the form of law, which represented his interests. It must be remembered, however, that despite slaves' inherent rightlessness and no matter what ideal expectations of servile deference and obedience owners entertained, slavery itself always remained a form of *compulsory* labour, which implies two things : on one hand the unwillingness of slaves to remain in servitude if an alternative were available, and on the other hand the need for owners to exercise continuous coercion, of one kind or another, if slaves were to remain socially content and economically productive. It was characteristic of slaves as human property that they were able to demonstrate human reaction to and even opposition against their condition of inferiority, and evidence of such behaviour has been seen. It may also have been essential for slaves' own survival that they accommodate themselves to their condition [3], but such accommodation was also required by slave-owners in order that their world of privilege might be sustained, and it cannot be allowed that servile accommodation was an automatic, natural sequel to

---

(1) FINLEY (1973), 67ff. ; (1980), 68ff.
(2) See references at p. 25 n. 23, and cf. also FINLEY (1980), 77 ; 104.
(3) FINLEY (1980), 116.

the mere state of enslavement ; instead accommodation had to be elicited by catering to slaves' interests or imposed by overriding them. In spite of the diversity of slave statuses in the Roman slavery system, therefore, and in spite of the absence of overt class consciousness among slaves, it was the case that deliberately contrived methods of controlling and manipulating them were obligatory on the part of the ruling classes. Roman slave-owners were well aware of this reality, and the information of the Roman writers on agriculture particularly implies that control of slave property was impossible without conscious effort on their part to that end.

In view of the restrictions outlined at the outset of this essay any conclusions arrived at must remain tentative, even hypothetical. But from the certain framework that slaves in Roman society were varyingly the recipients of generous and not so generous forms of treatment from their owners, certain observations, at least, can be presented. First, and on one basic level, it seems that the life of the slave alternated between rewards and punishments which depended on the proclivities of individual slave-owners. Immediate rewards such as holidays and privileges of a deeper significance such as the capacity to establish and maintain a family or to aspire towards and achieve manumission were offset by slaves' periodic subjection to physical pain and suffering. It follows from this state of affairs that the slave was never able to take anything for granted, so that in consequence his submission to and acquiescence before the owner were guaranteed : rewards and privileges provided incentives towards compliant industry, punishment added the spur when necessary and quite literally beat down the slave's independence. In many respects, therefore, it could be said that the greater the slave's compliance to the will of his owner the better the conditions of his life would become ; greater lenience and fewer doses of the lash could be expected in proportion to the degree of demonstrated and observed loyalty and obedience. At this level control of the Roman slave population and continuation of the Roman slavery system were made possible through the maintenance by owners of a balance between generosity and its opposite towards slaves, a balance of which recognition clearly appears in Columella's statement, which may be presumed to be typical in thought of Columella's peers, that control of subordinates requires avoidance by superiors of excessive indulgence and of excessive cruelty [4]. Admittedly much of the physical violence in slave

(4) Col. *RR*. 11.1.25.

life seems to have been capriciously inflicted, erratic and lacking in justification ; and the granting of freedom, especially by will, might also have been equally arbitrary. But at the same time enough evidence survives to make clear that privileges and punishments were consciously recognised and consciously employed as vehicles of social control, even if individual slave-owners at times overstepped the limits of what was utilitarian in their application of them.

Secondly, however, beyond this mechanism of alternating treatment and at a far more abiding level there is another observable aspect which governed the servile mentality. The rewards and privileges which masters allowed their slaves were not all of equal value : a distinction obviously existed between the single concession of a brief holiday and those of maintaining a family or being granted freedom from servitude. No slave was about to find his life irreparably shattered if an anticipated period of release from work were suddenly denied him by his owner for whatever reason (though he may have been temporarily irked). But because family life and liberty were of considerable importance to slaves, to judge from the evidence which is available, the emotional distress and suffering are likely to have been enormous at those times when the slave found his family involuntarily broken up or if freedom which had been promised him were suddenly and arbitrarily closed off. It has been contended that servile family life and the path towards the acquisition of freedom were surrounded by a number of adversative factors beyond the immediate control of the slave which rendered security in slave life minimal. The prospect of sale among slave family members was a particular constant cause of anxiety, and the actual conferment of freedom on slaves was relatively uncommon. In order to protect privileges already acquired, therefore, or in the hope of gaining them, it might be said that the safest policy for slaves was to comply with and conform to the wishes of their owners, the product being the semblance of harmony between slave and master or continuing social stability between slave and free. Because slaves knew the hardships and dangers which characterised their familial lives and their pursuit of freedom, the element of fear which they experienced from the amount of physical abuse and violence in their relationships with their owners extended also, and penetrated deeply into the enjoyment of privileges they had been conceded. Under these circumstances masters' potential for psychological domination over their slave property was intensified beyond that which stemmed from the simple, but arbitrary fluctuation between kindliness and severity.

Since no accounts written by slaves of their experiences during slavery exist, the extent of this posited emotional factor in servile life cannot be adequately evaluated. It is not capable of measurement. But some support is available in the form of analogy, even though analogy cannot be used as absolute proof in and of itself for the generally bleak conditions of Roman slaves which have been suggested. Nonetheless it has been proposed from a purely psychological perspective that the existence of a predominant climate of fear and the use of coercive power by a superior on a subordinate may well lead to compliant and submissive behaviour in the subordinate, perhaps of childlike quality, and, given his will to survive adversity, even to an adoption by him of the superior's values, although within this corporate response there may be great variations of behaviour from individual to individual [5]. This theory was proposed by a historian of slavery in the New World, and far more elaborately than the crude summary statement just given, in an effort to explain the conventional image of the black slave as Sambo held by slave-owners in the Southern states of America. The argument depended in part on a psychological study of prisoners-of-war in Nazi concentration camps, where a submissiveness and docility akin to putative features of the black slave personality were visible. Among modern historians this view has generated intense debate, not yet over, which has included vigorous attack and denial, on the grounds for example that the comparison of the concentration camps was defective or that one predominant image of black slaves in the United States never existed [6]. Yet with due allowance being made for overstatement and due caution being invoked, something useful for what has been seen of the experiences of slaves in the Roman world may still be salvaged from the essential hypothesis.

---

(5) Stanley M. ELKINS, *Slavery : A Problem in American Institutional and Intellectual Life*[3], Chicago, 1976, 81ff. ; the book first appeared in 1959. Cf. John W. BLASSINGAME, *The Slave Community : Plantation Life in the Antebellum South*[2], New York, 1979, 284ff. ; first published in 1972.

(6) The literature on modern slavery which has appeared since, and in response to Elkins is immense ; for a survey of developments see D. B. DAVIS, *Slavery and the Post-World War II Historians* in *Daedalus* 103 (1974), 1ff., as well as Elkins' own treatment in chapter six of the third edition of his book (above, n. 5). A collection of papers which discuss Elkins' views appear in Ann J. LANE, ed., *The Debate over Slavery : Stanley Elkins and his Critics*, Urbana, 1971. Cf. also M. I. FINLEY, *Slavery and the Historians* in *Histoire sociale / Social History* 12 (1979), 247ff ; Kenneth M. STAMPP, *The Imperilled Union*, New York, 1982, 164ff.

In the imperial period of Roman history slaves did not, as far as can be told, organise a great number of revolts or commit a great number of violent acts against their owners. Instead, on the surface at least fidelity was more forthcoming than not. This situation, however, cannot be taken as an index of slaves' true, inner thoughts and feelings, in the sense that they can automatically be assumed to have been satisfied with their social inferiority and were in consequence content to display undivided loyalty to their owners for its own sake (though some undoubtedly were). Rather, as a result of the fears and anxieties which conditioned the life of slaves as described earlier, it may be suggested that the role of the slave desired by the slave-owner became internalised within him to such a degree that it created the response of apparent obedience, variously sincere or disguised according to the individual slave's wish to safeguard himself and his privileges and to preserve some sense of individuality through means of resistance less obvious and dangerous than those of overt rebellion. If this is right, the leverage for manipulation and exploitation which thereby accrued to the slave-owner was immense.

There must be no confusion here. No suggestion is being made that slaves in Roman society did not, in significantly large numbers and over time, successfully enjoy family life or acquire release from slavery and other privileges. It is plainly the case that they did. Nor should it be doubted that these privileges occasionally followed from the benign interest of slave-owners in their slaves. But until the slave had obtained freedom, and in the case of those with families until freedom was acquired for the full group, there could not be any guarantee, even for those slaves in the most favourable circumstances, of release from the climate of fear which characterised the period of actual enslavement in an all-embracing manner. Above all, therefore, it is this absence of psychological and emotional security in slave life which offers the key to understanding the continuing ability of Roman slave-owners to control and keep in subjection their slaves. The capacity of masters to control the minds of their slaves contributes, so it may be proposed, to explaining the endurance of slavery across time within the Roman world.

APPENDICES

A. The biography of Columella constructed by C. Cichorius (*Römische Studien*, Stuttgart, 1922, 411ff.) remains standard ; cf. *PIR*² I 779 ; Griffin (1976), 89, 290f. Of the few known facts of his life, Columella's Spanish origin has been grossly overvalued in attempts to tie him to L. Annaeus Seneca. On one view Columella was an 'adepte de Sénèque', 'qu'il admira avec ferveur', belonged to a politico-literary group headed by Seneca, and attended meetings given by Seneca's nephew, Lucan (Cizek (1972), 61, 128, 290, 370 ; cf. also Martin (1971), 290, 363). Less extreme but equally tenuous are the suggestions that Columella may have 'sought out' Seneca when he came to Rome and that Seneca acted as Columella's literary patron (Griffin (1976), 253 ; 290f. ; cf. *JRS* 62 (1972), 1ff.). The sole item of firm evidence on which such views depend is Columella's polite description of Seneca as *uir excellentis ingenii atque doctrinae* (*RR*. 3.3.3). Seneca's brother, L. Iunius Gallio, is also mentioned by Columella (*RR*. 9.16.2) in such a way as to leave no doubt that he did act as Columella's patron. But the terms of reference are quite distinct : Gallio is *Gallio noster*, as *M. Trebellius noster* (*RR*. 5.1.2), whereas the notice on Seneca is formal and purely passing. It does not seem enough on which to build a close relationship between Columella and Seneca.

B. The major slave wars which occurred in Sicily and Italy between 140 B.C. and 70 B.C. are important events because of their general exceptionality. Although the source material for these events is notoriously full of difficulties, one undoubted aspect of the exceptionality is the eventual scale of the risings : vast numbers of slaves became involved, and the dangers they posed to established society were genuine. But the rebels did not formulate any specific, programmatic goals which they hoped to implement, other than their own escape from slavery. 'The slave revolts of the ancient world ... struggled for some kind of perceived restoration and lacked the material base and concomitant ideology for the projection of a new and economically more advanced society' (E. D. Genovese, *From Rebellion to Revolution*, Baton Rouge and London, 1979, 82). It is sometimes maintained that the slaves in Sicily set up hellenistic styled kingdoms (on the particular model of the Seleucids ; see especially Vogt (1975), 39ff. ; cf. Milani (1972), 197f.), their object being 'to invert society' (Vogt (1975), 54 ; cf. 58f.). But the organisation which is visible in the account (mainly) of Diodorus Siculus should not be regarded in my view as an object in and of itself, only as a means of maintaining the momentum of rebellion once escalation of numbers had started to occur. In all three wars events began on a low scale. In the first Sicilian revolt, a small number of slaves looked to the Syrian wonderworker Eunus for sanction of their murderous revenge against a single master, Damophilus, in one household (Diod. Sic. 34/5.2.10-11 ; Florus, 2.7.4ff., attributes outbreak of rebellion solely to Eunus and has no mention of Damophilus ; Diodorus (34/5.2.4 ; 37) mentions slave discussions of revolt and murder before the actual outbreak, but no careful planning on the grandscale is indicated ; it should not be odd that slaves at any time discussed the *idea* of revolt). In the second episode Diodorus tells of revolts in two households, but there is no sign of coordination between them (Diod. Sic. 36.3.4-6 ; 4.1-2 ; cf. Florus, 2.7.9ff. ; respectively thirty and eighty slaves were involved). Spartacus' rebellion, finally, began with two hundred gladiators' resentment of their status, and when plans for escape were betrayed, a successful break was made by some seventy-eight of them (Plut. *Crassus* 9.4 ; cf. Livy, *Per.* 95 ; App. *BC* 1.116). This suggests strongly that the early rebels did not intend their actions to expand in the way that happened, rather that their initial successes sparked off the widespread potential for rebellion that always existed. Important factors in this were the first-generation nature of many of the slaves, their common geographic origins, and the emergence of competent leaders who were able to impose some organisation on the rebels (though Spartacus quickly lost control). It should not be surprising that the principals assumed the trappings of kingship in order to assist the process of organisation, but this does not indicate any programme of long-term import based on political ideology and with the prime object of raising grandscale rebellion. The rebel leaders used whatever means were at their disposal to maintain order among the snowballing numbers of their adherents, means which were influenced (but no more, and not unexpectedly) by the established institutions with which they were familiar (cf. Diod. Sic. 36.2.2ff. on T. Minucius ; and C. L. R. James, *The Black Jacobins*, New York, 1963 edition, 93f. on Toussaint L'Ouverture). Yet there is no basis for believing that a great proliferation of slave numbers, which automatically invited the predictable response of Roman military retaliation, was sought by those responsible for the initial outbursts ; instead, the accidentally acquired strength of rebel numbers became their ultimate (and fatal) weakness.

C. According to Plutarch (*Cato* 21.2) it was the elder Cato's practice to charge his male slaves a fee for the privilege of entering the quarters of his female slaves and to confine servile relationships within his own household. The intention was to prevent disaffection among the slaves ; but the anecdote suggests that slaves' needs for sexual release, if not for the establishment of families, was recognised by slave-owners from an early point in the history of Roman slavery. Moreover, the contemporary evidence of Plautus gives some basis for believing that slave families were indeed in existence in Cato's day, if it can continue to be assumed that a realistic basis underlies Plautus' comedies. At *Amph.* 365, for example, the slave Sosia is able to identify his father ; at *Capt.* 888 the slave Stalagmus refers to his wife (*uxor* ; cf. also *Miles* 1008 ; *Stich.* 433 ; and for *uernae* note *Rud.* 218 ;

Miles 699). Note that Cato's wife is said to have nursed the children of her slaves herself (Plut. *Cato* 20.3 τὰ τῶν δούλων παιδάρια).

The frequency, however, with which slaves were able to enter into familial relationships in the mid Republic was obviously governed by the numbers of slave women available to serve as wives for male slaves. The huge importations of war captives in Rome's expansionist era are usually assumed to have consisted overwhelmingly of men (e.g. Harris (1979), 84 n. 2), an assumption which must be essentially correct : slaves were required most of all to replace Italian peasants consumed by warfare and men were far more suitable for the purpose than women. Yet there are several indications that slave women were not as rare as is conventionally imagined. The story above about Cato shows clearly enough that he owned female domestics and Cato can hardly have been unique in this respect. References to female slave quarters at Plaut. *Most.* 756, 758, 908 suggest that Cato's practice of sexual segregation may not have been unique, whereas the expectation that slave women should form part of a domestic entourage is clear from *Miles* 1339. Again according to Plutarch (*Cato* 21.1) Cato habitually bought young slaves on the open market to be trained in domestic service, and these may have comprised girls as well as boys (as too the infants nursed by his wife) : Plaut. *Epid.* 43 contains a reference to the acquisition of a female slave *ex praeda* and *Epid.* 210f. a reference to the return of soldiers from campaign with male and female slaves in tow (cf. *Merc.* 415 for Syrian and Egyptian women). Moreover, the list of traditional female slave occupations at Plaut. *Merc.* 396ff. (weaving, grinding grain, cutting wood, spinning, house cleaning, cooking for the *familia*, cf. 509, shepherding) can be nothing but a reflection of historical circumstance (cf. Brunt (1971), 144) and the ubiquitous appearance in Plautus of female slave-prostitutes and of kidnapped women should not be attributed to literary convention alone.

It must be accepted that in all probability some slaves did reproduce in the earliest phase of Rome's developed slavery system, which means in turn that female as well as male infants will have appeared in the next generation (cf. Watson (1968), 291ff. on the acceptance of such by Republican jurists). Although the issue of infant female exposure has to be taken into consideration, it would be nonsense to assume that some females were not raised for domestic service at least, females who would in due course provide wives for slave men on reaching adulthood. It may be the case that there were more females in domestic occupations in cities than in the country at large and that the possibilities for slave family life were better in cities in consequence. Even so, there is no reason why Treggiari's view that certain numbers of infant females were sifted off from the city to be raised on farms (see above, p. 76) should not be applied retroactively for the age of Cato. The comparatively low level of fertility in the Roman slave population is not to be attributed alone to the insufficiency of slave women for purposes of reproduction.

D. For more than forty years the standard account of Augustus' social programme has been that of Last, and of necessity something was said about the slavery legislation (Last (1934), 429 ff.). Because Last's views have been so influential, and because they are not followed here, it may be of value to describe them in some detail and to show their impact in subsequent scholarly work.

A single thread, essentially, runs through Last's account : the Romans' need to avoid contamination of their stock by excessive manumission of Eastern slaves. Emphasis was put on the double danger of too many manumissions and of the pollution of the Roman and Italian peoples by Eastern elements − hence a racial theme and a numerical theme. 'If the population of Italy was only maintained by immigration, it must soon become a nondescript farrago, with the Roman element too weak to leaven the whole lump'. Thus Augustus 'was involved in measures which, by arresting the extension of the Roman *ciuitas* and above all by setting limits to the numbers of those Greeks and Orientals who, coming to Italy as slaves, were merged on manumission into the general body of Roman citizens, would preserve that material from uncontrolled contamination' (Last (1934), 429). Last wrote of 'the threat made to the character of the Roman people by the numbers in which slaves were set free' ; of damning 'one of the broadest channels by which foreign blood flowed into the community of Roman citizens' ; and of 'the infiltration of foreign blood' being 'brought under control' by legislation (Last (1934), 432 ; 433 ; 464). Although other factors were considered, these quotations reflect Last's principal ideas.

Before Last, Duff showed the same concern for the numbers and racial origins of manumitted slaves (Duff (1958), 30ff. ; cf. Last (1934), 949). But Last's influence in particular has been extensive. Thus R. Syme (*The Roman Revolution*, Oxford, 1939, 446), speaking of Rome's 'readiness to admit new members to the citizen body' in Republican history, spelled out the 'grave' result that 'slaves not only could be emancipated with ease but were emancipated in hordes. The wars of conquest flooded the market with captives of alien and often inferior stocks ... Augustus stepped in to save the race, imposing severe restriction upon the freedom of individual owners in liberating their slaves'. Less emotively H. H. Scullard (*From the Gracchi to Nero*[4], London, 1976, 240 unchanged since the first edition of 1959) wrote that 'Augustus wished not only to increase the Italian element in the Roman citizen body, but also to limit the foreign element that was mixing with it, especially as a result of manumission'. And Jones (1970), 133, wrote of the 'excessive and indiscriminate manumission of slaves, or rather the massive influx of freed slaves into the citizen body' as a 'social problem' confronting Augustus. (Cf. also Westermann (1955), 89f. ; Crook (1967), 43).

The connection between and insistence on numbers and race has continued down to the present with little sustained questioning, though Brunt (1958), 164 briefly stresses the incentive of full freedom for reasons to do with economic efficiency rather than with social harmony ; cf. also E. M. Staerman, *Die Blütezeit der Sklavenwirtschaft in der römischen Republik*, Wiesbaden, 1969, 274f., who sees the Augustan laws as an attempt to soften the relations between the free and unfree urban plebs, relations that were dangerous to the ruling classes (but the laws were not restricted to Rome alone) ; and Burford (1972), 50, who suggests that Augustus wished to protect heirs' interests with the *lex Fufia* (which takes no account of the *lex Aelia*). Yet the conventional account raises difficulties. For example, what evidence is there that Augustus really feared racial contamination of the Roman body politic ; that he was ill-disposed to its assimilation of Eastern or any foreign elements ; or that he believed slaves were being set free in excessive numbers ? Recent scholarship suggests, in fact, no sign of racial antipathy from Augustus towards Greeks and the Greek world (G. W. Bowersock, *Augustus and the Greek World* (1965), 41 ; 61) and that racial prejudice, as currently understood, was a notion scarcely visible in antiquity (A. N. Sherwin-White, *Racial Prejudice in Imperial Rome*, Cambridge, 1967). Extension of the citizenship to peregrine communities under Augustus is well established (Sherwin-White (1973), 225 ff.). And, while precise measurement is impossible, there is no justification for assuming a glut of Greek and Oriental slaves at Rome in the Augustan era to overwhelm the state (see E. S. Gruen, *The Last Generation of the Roman Republic*, Berkeley and Los Angeles, 1974, 360f. with references to earlier work). Last did not consider other sources of slave supply immediately before Augustus' legislation, nor did he provide direct evidence for his theory of racial contamination. And too much emphasis was put on Dionysius, at least as interpreted above.

E. According to Livy (7.16.7) the *uicesima libertatis* was instituted in 357 B.C. at a time when the senate was anxious to create a new source of public revenue, since the reserves of the *aerarium Saturni* were depleted. By 209 B.C. (Livy 27.10.11-12) some four thousand pounds of gold had accumulated from the proceeds of the tax, although there is no way of telling how long it had taken for the reserve to build up, or the number of manumissions thereby represented (cf. Brunt (1971), 549 f. ; Westermann (1955), 71). Cicero has a passing reference to the tax (*Att.* 2.16.1 ; 59 B.C.), whose proceeds Caesar may have drawn on ten years later (Brunt (1971), 549f.), but otherwise little else is heard of the *uicesima* under the Republic. Subsequently Caracalla is reported to have doubled the tax, Macrinus to have quickly restored it to its original level (Dio 77.9.4 ; 78.12.2). The common view is that the *uicesima* survived until the age of Diocletian and Constantine, whose fiscal reforms brought about its demise as an independent tax (e.g. Cagnat (1882), 156 ; Hirschfeld (1905), 109 ; *RE* 8 col. 2478 (G. Wesener)). But this can no longer be certain in view of *P. Mich.* 462 (as restored by J. F. Gilliam, *AJP* 71 (1950), 437f. = *CPL* no. 171), which, whether pre- or post-Constantinian, provides evidence of continued collection of the tax in fourth century Egypt, and renders invalid the view that 'In the second century, when the number of slaves decreased, the tax dwindled to unimportant dimensions' (Frank (1940), 50).

Detailed knowledge of the organisation of the *uicesima* cannot be obtained from literary sources. Livy (27.10.11-12) says that proceeds were maintained *in sanctiore aerario*, and scholars have assumed only for emergency purposes, as in 209 B.C. (thus Cagnat (1882), 154 ; Frank (1940), 50 ; Westermann (1955), 71 ; Cl. Nicolet, *Le Métier de citoyen dans la Rome républicaine*, Paris, 1976, 230) ; but this is in fact unlikely ; see Brunt (1971), 549f. The tax was sometimes paid by slaves, sometimes by their masters (Epict. *Diss.* 2.1.26 ; 4.1.33 ; Petr. *Sat.* 5.8.2 ; 71.2) ; hence the theory that the *uicesima* was paid by the slave if he bought his freedom following agreement with his owner, but by the owner if freedom was granted as a generosity, for example by testament (Cagnat (1882), 168ff. ; A. Berger, *An Encyclopedic Dictionary of Roman Law*, Philadelphia, 1953, s.v. 'vicesima manumissionum' ; for unambiguous cases of testamentary provision of the *uicesima* see *FIRA*² III no. 48 lines 53-4 ; no. 47 lines 36-7). But it remains uncertain when such a convention developed, and whether it was ever legally ratified.

Inscriptional evidence indicates the predictable : that in the late Republic and early Empire the *uicesima* was farmed out to the *publicani* (e.g. *CIL* 11. 5435 ; 5.164 ; 10.3875), and that under the Empire its administration eventually fell within the purview of the emperor (see *RE* Supp. 6 col. 1034 (Westermann) for a *procurator XX libertatis* before 79). For a time *publicani* and imperial procurators must have collected the tax contemporaneously (cf. *CIL* 3.7729 with Dessau *ad ILS* 4241 ; *CIL* 3.6753 with Weaver (1972), 57 ; 3.4827 with *PIR*² A 1469), which is not impossible ; cf. Millar (1977), 624f. Reorganisation by Septimius Severus also seems likely ; see H.-G. Pflaum, *Les Carrières procuratoriennes équestres sous le haut-empire romain*, Paris, 1960, 94f. On the assumption that their find-spots reflect activity in those areas, inscriptions reveal collection of the *uicesima* on an empire wide basis in the imperial period ; see *CIL* 5.3351 ; 2.4187 ; 12.2396 ; 3.6753 ; 3.7729 ; 3.7287 ; 13.7215 ; 8.7099 ; *AE* 1930 no. 87 ; add *P. Oxy.* 2265 to *CPL* no. 171 for Egypt. The history of the *uicesima libertatis* is worth further treatment.

F. At *Fab.* III prol. 33-37, Phaedrus accounts for the origin of the fable as follows :

> *Nunc, fabularum cur sit inuentum genus,*
> *breui docebo. seruitus obnoxia,*
> *quia quae uolebat non audebat dicere,*
> *affectus proprios in fabellas transtulit,*
> *calumniamque fictis elusit iocis.*

Seruitus here might mean servitude of any kind, such as political servitude under a despotic form of government (e.g. the Principate, the sense understood by J. Wight Duff, *A Literary History of Rome in the Silver Age*³, London, 1964, 113f. and *Roman Satire* (Berkeley and Los Angeles, 1936, 110). But the word may equally mean the condition of being a slave, which would then suggest that the origin of the fable should be ascribed to slaves and stories told by them in such a way that the true meaning was disguised so as to spare slaves punishment from their masters. If true this explanation would be of great importance, especially in view of the prevailing absence of a slave literature in antiquity, because it would point to the existence of an oral form of servile protest otherwise unknown. Can the explanation be accepted as plausible ?

The fable has an extremely long history in the ancient world and the question of its origins cannot be resolved by recourse to one determining factor (for the complications see K. Meuli, *Herkunft und Wesen der Fabel, Gesammelte Schriften*, Basel/Stuttgart, 1975, II 731ff. ; M. Nøjgaard, *La Fable antique I*, Copenhagen, 1964 ; B. E. Perry, *Introduction* to the Loeb edition of Babrius and Phaedrus (1975)). Moreover, it is clear from the hints of literary pretension that Phaedrus did not address himself solely, if at all, to a servile audience, and many of his fables have no relevance, by any stretch of the imagination, to servile situations.

On the other hand Phaedrus himself had of course been a slave before, as an imperial freedman, he turned to the literary composition of fables, and so might be presumed to have had an interest in any expression of servile points of view. And there is no reason simply to dismiss out of hand the notion that the fable could function as a vehicle of servile protest and indirect criticism of slave-owners, whether at a very early date, in Phaedrus' own lifetime, or beyond ; indeed, fables have served this purpose in other slave societies (cf. E. D. Genovese, *Roll, Jordan, Roll*, Vintage ed. New York, 1976, 582). The subject has apparently received little attention from scholars, though Daube (1972), 53ff. has accepted the reality of slave stories contributing to the tradition of the fable and has pointed to two examples from Phaedrus which fit the context of servile protest (making allowance at the same time for embellishment by the author himself) : in *Fab*. I.15 Daube sees a 'rather hefty incitement to disloyalty, to not caring a hoot' and in *App. Per*. 17 a 'recommendation of deceitfulness'. Cf. also M. Nøjgaard, *La Fable antique II*, Copenhagen, 1967, pp. 174 ff.

The explanation is thus plausible, and the question naturally arises of whether other fables told by Phaedrus seem suitable for explication along the lines of servile protest or statement. The following are examples which, without too great an imposition on credulity, appear consistent with themes and subjects dealt with in this study.

1. I.6 : Jupiter enquires why the Frogs are upset at the prospect of the Sun's marriage ; he is told that the Sun dries up the Frogs' pond as it is and causes their deaths ; so what will happen when the Sun procreates ? This fable fits the background of slaves' fears of masters' cruelty, and may be taken as an expression of slaves' anxieties about the coming to maturity of owners' children and the additional threats of abuse they represent.

2. I.8 : a Crane and a Wolf strike a bargain for the extraction of a bone from the Wolf's throat ; once the Crane has performed the operation, the Wolf refuses to pay up, claiming the Crane was lucky not to have had its head bitten off beforehand. This is reminiscent of the striking of compacts between slave and master for manumission, as in the Pedanius Secundus affair (above pp. 99ff. and cf. Plaut. *Pers*. 192), on which the master always might renege, and the use of a potential reward as an inducement to compliance is also noticeable. The fable expresses the slave's realisation that a slave-owner cannot, ultimately, be trusted, and that a trusting slave only harms himself.

3. I.28 : an Eagle carries off a Fox's cubs as food for her young ; the Fox seeks the cubs' release but is rebuffed by the Eagle ; the Fox then prepares to burn the tree which houses the Eagle's nest, and under the threat of losing her own young the Eagle returns the cubs. This story suits the context of slaves being separated from family members at the dictate of the master, and threatens retaliatory violence in a manner which obviously could not be stated openly but which might nonetheless make slave-owners aware of the dangers to themselves from slaves if pushed too far (cf. above pp. 113f.) : *Quamuis sublimes debent humiles metuere, / uindicta docili quia patet sollertiae*. Yet given the real problems slaves faced in taking vengeance against owners (cf. above pp. 31f.), and the common fact of family separation among slaves, the story may have functioned more as a consolation for slaves rather than as an expression of true intent. The same is true of II.16, which is on the same theme, an individual's *superbia* and lack of *humanitas* towards others may lead to his discomfiture. Here the agricultural writers' recognition of the need for kindly treatment of slaves may be compared, together with the stereotype of the cruel master represented by Larcius Macedo (above p. 121). The 'craftiness' common to I.28 and III.16 recalls the type of the cunning slave (above pp. 28f.).

4. II.8 : a hunted Stag takes refuge in an ox-stall on a farm ; it goes unnoticed by the *bubulcus*, other *rustici*, and even the *uilicus* ; but when the farm owner (*dominus*) arrives to inspect his cattle, he first notices signs of servile neglect – insufficient fodder and bedding for the animals, cobwebs everywhere – and then discovers the Stag, which is killed before the assembled *familia*. The point of the fable, *dominum uidere plurimum in rebus suis*, is especially appropriate for a servile audience as a reminder of the need to beware the master ; but the references to dilatoriness echo complaints of slovenliness seen elsewhere (above pp. 27f.) and so reflect slaves' recognition of their ability to cause the owner annoyance, at least, which provides humour in the re-telling of the story among them. Perhaps a satirical note is directed towards the *dominus*.

5. III.7 : in return for his vigilance as a nightwatchman, a Dog is well fed by his master (*dominus*) and has a place to live ; during the daytime, however, he is chained up, has no freedom of movement, and his neck bears the mark of his collar ; a Wolf rejects the offer of joining the Dog's household, preferring his

liberty, even at the cost of hunger and no shelter. The point of this fable, *quam dulcis sit libertas*, has obvious relevance to slave circumstances and slaves' aspirations towards freedom (cf. above, p. 82), but its details recall the use of slave collars and the *ergastulum* as well. The story, from the servile point of view, is a lament that the material comforts of slavery do not compensate the absence of freedom. An expression of such dissatisfaction, however, clearly could not be articulated openly.

6. IV.4 : Boar and a Horse are involved in a dispute ; the Horse secures the aid of a Man, who kills the Boar but then reduces the Horse to slavery (*seruitus*) ; the moral, *inpune potius laedi quam dedi alteri*. This has application to the process by which a slave might secure redress against injury done to himself by the master from a magistrate (cf. above, pp. 123ff.), and can be understood as a protest against the inequity of the legal system which merely handed over the slave to a new owner if his case were upheld, or else as a consolation, since it was scarcely worthwhile to seek help. Cf. I.15, which could be taken to mean that one slave-owner is no better than another and that nothing is to be gained from the 'award' of a new master. Cf. also I.30, a fatalistic response to the civil wars of the Late Republic ?

7. V.10 : a Hunting-Dog, always successful and efficient in the past, is now too old to work for its Master (*dominus*) ; after failing to secure a boar, the Dog is reprimanded, but puts up a spirited self-defence : *Non te destituit animus, sed uires meae. / quod fuimus lauda, si iam damnas quod sumus.* This fable is particularly interesting because Phaedrus does not explain its meaning, claiming that the significance is obvious. It recalls the sources which speak of the abandonment by owners of old and sickly slaves (though contrast Columella's recommendation of good medical treatment ; above p. 22), and may be understood as the response of slaves to the onset of old age and the fear of abandonment it brought. The story is a statement to the slave-owner that long years of loyalty should be rewarded with humane treatment when high work performance can no longer be maintained. Perhaps defiantly so.

The ideas expressed about these fables do not prove that the fable had servile origins or that the fables themselves circulated among slaves or spoke to servile circumstances. The viability of a fable depends after all on its applicability to many and different situations. But without undue strain, the applicability to slave circumstances of the fables referred to above is fairly clear, which supports the view that fables were at least influenced by forms of slave protest-statements.

SELECT BIBLIOGRAPHY

This list contains works cited more than once ; full details of other items will be found in the notes.

ALFÖLDY, G. (1972), *Die Freilassung von Sklaven und die Struktur der Sklaverei in der römischen Kaiserzeit* in *RSA* 2, 97-129.

ASTIN, A. E. (1978), *Cato the Censor*, Oxford.

ATKINSON, Kathleen M. T. (1966), *The Purpose of the Manumission Laws of Augustus* in *The Irish Jurist* 1, 356-374.

BALSDON, J. P. V. D. (1969), *Life and Leisure in Ancient Rome*, London.

BARBU, N. I. (1963), *Les Esclaves chez Martial et Juvenal* in *Acta Antiqua Philippopolitana*, Serdica, 67-74.

BELLEN, H. (1971), *Studien zur Sklavenflucht in römischen Kaiserreich*, Wiesbaden.

BIEZUNSKA-MAŁOWIST, I. M. (1969), *Les Enfants-esclaves à la lumière des papyrus* in *Hommages à Marcel Renard, Collection Latomus* 101, II, Brussels, 91-96.

BIEZUNSKA-MAŁOWIST, I. M. (1973a) *L'Esclavage dans l'Egypte gréco-romaine* in *Actes du Colloque 1971 sur l'esclavage*, Paris, 81-92.

BIEZUNSKA-MAŁOWIST, I. M. (1973b), *L'Opinion que les anciens avaient du travail servile* in F. C. LANE, ed., *Fourth International Congress of Economic History, Bloomington, 1968*, 366-372.

BIEZUNSKA-MAŁOWIST, I. M. (1975), *La Traite d'esclaves en Egypte* in *Proceedings of the XIV International Congress of Papyrologists*, London, 11-18.

BIEZUNSKA-MAŁOWIST, I. M. (1976), *L'Esclavage à Alexandrie dans la période gréco-romaine* in *Actes du Colloque 1973 sur l'esclavage*, Paris, 293-312.

BIEZUNSKA-MAŁOWIST, I. M. (1977), *L'Esclavage dans l'Egypte gréco-romaine, Seconde Partie : Période romaine*, Wroclaw.

BODOR, A. (1963), *Dacian Slaves and Freedmen in the Roman Empire* in *Acta Antiqua Philippolitana*, Serdica, 45-52.

BOULVERT, G. (1970), *Esclaves et affranchis impériaux sous le haut-empire romain*, Naples.

BOYER, Laurent (1965), *La Fonction sociale des legs d'après la jurisprudence classique* in *RD* 43, 333-408.

BRADLEY, K. R. (1980), *Sexual Regulations in Wet-Nursing Contracts from Roman Egypt* in *Klio* 62, 321-325.

BRAUN, Pierre (1959), *Les Tabous des "Feriae"* in *L'Année sociologique*[3], 49-125.

BROCKMEYER, N. (1968), *Arbeitsorganisation und ökonomisches Denken in der Gutwirtschaft des römischen Reiches*, Bochum.

BRUNT, P. A. (1958), Review of Westermann (1955), *JRS* 48, 164-170.

BRUNT, P. A. (1971), *Italian Manpower*, Oxford.

BRUNT, P. A. (1973), *Aspects of the Social Thought of Dio Chrysostom and of the Stoics* in *PCPhS* 19², 9-34.

BUCKLAND, W. W. (1908), *The Roman Law of Slavery*, Cambridge.

BURFORD, Alison (1972), *Craftsmen in Greek and Roman Society*, London & Ithaca, N.Y.

BURTON, G. P. (1975), *Proconsuls, Assizes and the Administration of Justice under the Empire* in *JRS* 65, 92-106.

CAGNAT, M. R. (1882), *Etude historique sur les impôts indirects chez les Romains*, Paris.

CIZEK, E. (1972), *L'Epoque de Néron et ses controverses idéologiques*, Leiden.

CREȚIA, P. (1961), *Dion de Pruse et l'esclavage* in *StudClas* 3, 369-375.

CROOK, J. (1967), *Law and Life of Rome*, London & Ithaca, N.Y.

DAUBE, D. (1972), *Civil Disobedience in Antiquity*, Edinburgh.

DUFF, A. M. (1958), *Freedmen in the Early Roman Empire*, Cambridge.

DUNCAN-JONES, Richard (1974), *The Economy of the Roman Empire : Quantitative Studies*, Cambridge.

ENGELS, Donald (1980), *The Problem of Female Infanticide in the Greco-Roman World* in *CP* 75, 112-120.

FINLEY, M. I. (1973), *The Ancient Economy*, Berkeley & Los Angeles.

FINLEY, M. I. (1976), *A Peculiar Institution ?* in *Times Literary Supplement*, July 2, 819-821.

FINLEY, M. I. (1979), *Ancient Sicily to the Arab Conquest*, London (revised edition).

FINLEY, M. I. (1980), *Ancient Slavery and Modern Ideology*, New York.

FLORY, Marleen B. (1978), *Family in "Familia" : Kinship and Community in Slavery* in *AJAH* 3, 78-95.

FRANK, Tenney (1940), *An Economic Survey of Ancient Rome : Volume V, Rome and Italy of the Empire*, Baltimore.

GARNSEY, Peter (1970), *Social Status and Legal Privilege in the Roman Empire*, Oxford.

GRIFFIN, Miriam T. (1976), *Seneca : A Philosopher in Politics*, Oxford.

GSELL, ST. (1932), *Esclaves ruraux dans l'Afrique romaine* in *Mélanges Gustave Glotz* I, Paris, 397-415.

HARRIS, William V. (1979), *War and Imperialism in Republican Rome*, Oxford.

HARRIS, William V. (1980), *Towards a Study of the Roman Slave Trade* in *MAAR* 36, 117-140.

HIRSCHFELD, O. (1905), *Die Kaiserlichen Verwaltungsbeamten bis auf Diocletian²*, Berlin.

HOPKINS, Keith (1965), *The Age of Roman Girls at Marriage* in *Population Studies* 18, 309-327.

HOPKINS, Keith (1967), *Slavery in Classical Antiquity* in A. DE REUCK, J. KNIGHT edd., *Caste and Race : Comparative Approaches*, Boston, 166-191.

HOPKINS, Keith (1978), *Conquerors and Slaves : Sociological Studies in Roman History I*, Cambridge.

HOPKINS, Keith (1980), *Brother-Sister Marriage in Roman Egypt* in *Comparative Studies in Society and History* 22, 303-354.

JOHNSON, A. C. (1936), *Roman Egypt* = TENNEY FRANK ed., *An Economic Survey of Ancient Rome, Vol. II*, Baltimore.

JONES, A. H. M. (1968), *Slavery in the Ancient World* in *Economic History Review*² 9 (1956), 185-199 = M. I. FINLEY, ed., *Slavery in Classical Antiquity*, Cambridge & New York, 1-15.

JONES, A. H. M. (1970), *Augustus*, London.

JONES, C. P. (1978), *The Roman World of Dio Chrysostom*, Cambridge, Mass.

JONKERS, E. J. (1934), *De l'influence du Christianisme sur la législation relative à l'esclavage dans l'antiquité* in *Mnemosyne* 1, 241-280.

KAJANTO, I. (1969), *Tacitus on the Slaves* in *Arctos* 6, 43-60.

LAST, H. (1934), *The Social Policy of Augustus* in *CAH* X, 425-464.

LINTOTT, A. W. (1968), *Violence in Republican Rome*, Oxford.

MARÓTI, Egon (1976), *The Vilicus and the Villa-System in Ancient Italy* in *Oikumene* 1, 109-124.

MARTIN, R. (1971), *Recherches sur les agronomes latins et leurs conceptions économiques et sociales*, Paris.

MARTIN, R. (1974), *"Familia Rustica" : Les esclaves chez les agronomes latins* in *Actes du Colloque 1972 sur l'esclavage*, Paris, 267-297.

MILANI, Piero A. (1972), *La schiavitù nel pensiero politico dai greci al basso medio evo*, Milan.

MILLAR, Fergus (1977), *The Emperor in the Roman World*, London.

MONTEVECCHI, Orsolina (1973), *La papirologia*, Turin.

OATES, J. F. (1969), *Rhodian Auction Sale of a Slave Girl* in *JEA* 55, 191-210.

PIGANIOL, A. (1958), *Les Empereurs parlent aux esclaves* in *Romanitas* 1, 7-18 = *Collection Latomus* 133, Brussels, 1973, 202-211.

PLATNER, S. B. & ASHBY, T. A. (1929), *A Topographical Dictionary of Ancient Rome*, London.

RAWSON, Beryl (1966), *Family Life among the Lower Classes at Rome in the First Two Centuries of the Empire* in *CP* 61, 71-83.

RAWSON, Beryl (1974), *Roman Concubinage and Other De Facto Marriages* in *TAPA* 104, 279-305.

ROBLEDA, Olis (1976), *Il diritto degli schiavi nell'antica Roma*, Rome.

ROULAND, Norbert (1977), *A propos des servi publici populi Romani* in *Chiron* 7, 261-278.

SHERWIN-WHITE, A. N. (1966), *The Letters of Pliny : A Historical and Social Commentary*, Oxford.

SHERWIN-WHITE, A. N. (1973), *The Roman Citizenship²*, Oxford.

SPRANGER, P. P. (1961), *Historische Untersuchungen zu den Sklavenfiguren des Plautus und Terenz*, Wiesbaden.

STAERMAN, E. M. & TROFIMOVA, M. K. (1975), *La schiavitù nell'Italia imperiale*, Rome.

STE. CROIX, G. E. M. DE (1975), *Early Christian Attitudes towards Property and Slavery* in *Studies in Church History* 12, 1-38.

STRAUS, J. A. (1971), *Le Pays d'origine des esclaves de l'Egypte romaine* in *CE* 46, 363-366.

STRAUS, J. A. (1973), *Le Prix des esclaves dans les papyrus d'époque romaine* in *ZPE* 11, 289-295.

STRAUS, J. A. (1977), *Quelques activités exercées par les esclaves d'après les papyrus de l'Egypte romaine* in *Historia* 26, 74-88.

TAUBENSCHLAG, R. (1955), *The Law of Greco-Roman Egypt in the Light of the Papyri²*, Warsaw.

TREGGIARI, S. M. (1969), *Roman Freedmen during the Late Republic*, Oxford.

TREGGIARI, S. M. (1973), *Domestic Staff at Rome during the Julio-Claudian Period* in *Histoire sociale/ Social History* 6, 241-255.

TREGGIARI, S. M. (1975a), *Jobs in the Household of Livia* in *PBSR* 43, 48-77.

TREGGIARI, S. M. (1975b), *Family Life among the Staff of the Volusii* in *TAPA* 105, 393-401.

TREGGIARI, S. M. (1976), *Jobs for Women* in *AJAH* 1, 76-104.

TREGGIARI, S. M. (1979a), *Sentiment and Property : Some Roman Attitudes* in A. PAREL, T. FLANAGAN edd., *Theories of Property : Aristotle to the Present*, Waterloo, Ont., 53-85.

TREGGIARI, S. M. (1979b), *Questions on Women Domestics in the Roman West* in *Schiavitù, manomissione e classi dipendenti nel mondo antico*, (Università degli Studi di Padova, Pubblicazioni dell'instituto di storia antica 13), Rome, 185-201.

VEYNE, P. (1961), *Vie de Trimalcion* in *Annales* 16, 213-247.

VEYNE, P. (1978), *La Famille et l'amour sous le haut-empire romain* in *Annales* 33, 35-63.

VOGT, J. (1975), *Ancient Slavery and the Ideal of Man*, Cambridge, Mass.

VOLKMANN, Hans (1961), *Die Massenversklavungen der Einwohner eroberter Städte in der hellenistisch-römischen Zeit*, Wiesbaden.

WATSON, Alan (1968), *Morality, Slavery and the Jurists in the later Roman Republic* in *Tulane Law Review* 42, 289-303.

WATSON, Alan (1971), *Roman Private Law Around 200 B.C.*, Edinburgh.

WATSON, Alan (1975), *Rome of the XII Tables*, Princeton.

WEAVER, P. R. C. (1972), *Familia Caesaris*, Cambridge.

WESTERMANN, W. L. (1955), *The Slave Systems of Greek and Roman Antiquity*, Philadelphia.

WHITE, K. D. (1970), *Roman Farming*, London & Ithaca, N.Y.

WILLIAMS, G. W. (1958), *Some Aspects of Roman Marriage Ceremonies and Ideals* in *JRS* 48, 16-29.

WILLIAMS, G. W. (1968), *Tradition and Originality in Roman Poetry*, Oxford.

WILLIAMS, Wynne (1976), *Individuality in the Imperial Constitutions, Hadrian and the Antonines* in *JRS* 66, 67-83.

SUPPLEMENTARY BIBLIOGRAPHY

K.R. Bradley, 'Slave Kingdoms and Slave Rebellions in Ancient Sicily', *Historical Reflections/ Réflexions Historiques* 10 (1983), 435ff.

K.R. Bradley, 'Child Labour in the Roman World', *Historical Reflections/ Réflexions Historiques* 12 (1985), 311ff.

K.R. Bradley, 'Seneca and Slavery', *C&M* 37 (1986), 161ff.

J. Christes, 'Reflexe erlebter Unfreiheit in den Sentenzen des Publilius Syrus und in den Fabeln des Phaedrus. Zur Problematik ihrer Verifizierung', *Hermes* 107 (1979), 199ff.

Hervé Duchêne, 'Sur la Stèle d'Aulus Caprilius Timotheos, *Sômatemporos'*, *BCH* 110 (1986), 513ff.

Jane F. Gardner, *Women in Roman Law and Society* (London 1986).

M. Garrido-Hory, *Martial et l'esclavage* (Paris 1981).

Orlando Patterson, *Slavery and Social Death: A Comparative Study* (Cambridge, Mass. 1982).

Beryl Rawson, ed., *The Family in Ancient Rome: New Perspectives* (London 1986).

Olivia Robinson, 'Slaves and the Criminal Law', *ZSS Rom. Abt.* 98 (1981), 213ff.

A.J.B. Sirks, 'Informal Manumission and the Lex Junia', *RIDA* 28 (1981), 247ff.

A.J.B. Sirks, 'The *lex Junia* and the Effects of Informal Manumission and Iteration', *RIDA* 54 (1983), 211ff.

G.E.M. de Ste. Croix, *The Class Struggle in the Ancient Greek World* (Ithaca 1981).

Alan Watson, 'Roman Slave Law and Romanist Ideology', *Phoenix* 37 (1983), 53ff.

Thomas E.J. Wiedemann, 'The Regularity of Manumission at Rome', *CQ* 35 (1985), 162ff.

INDEX